Jewish Experience in the Art of the Twentieth Century

This exhibition has been made possible by grants from
The Joe and Emily Lowe Foundation
and the National Endowment for the Arts,
Washington, D.C., a Federal agency

October 16, 1975 through January 25, 1976

The Jewish Museum • New York

Published by The Jewish Museum, New York under the auspices of The Jewish Theological Seminary of America

Printed in the United States of America by Rumford Press Inc.
Design: Joseph del Gaudio at Design Farm.
© The Jewish Museum, New York, 1975

Library of Congress Catalog Card Number: 75-15212

Cover: **68. Marc Chagall.** *Time is a River without Banks (Le Temps n'a point de rive).* 1930-39. Oil on canvas. 39⅜ x 32 in. Collection The Museum of Modern Art, New York. Given anonymously, 1943.

Back cover: **95. Fritz Hundertwasser.** *House with Yellow Smoke.* 1962-63. Mixed media on paper. 31⅞ x 25⅝ in. Collection Susan T. and Joachim J. Aberbach, New York.

Contents

Lenders to the Exhibition

Susan T. and Joachim J. Aberbach, New York
Boris Aronson, Grandview, New York
David Aronson, Sudbury, Massachusetts
Menachem Bader, Kibbutz Mizra, Israel
Victor Barnett, New York
Tina and Shelomo Ben-Israel, New York
Yosl Bergner, Tel Aviv
Naftali Bezem, Jerusalem
Mrs. Olga Bineth, Jerusalem
Erich Brauer, Vienna
Mrs. Janet Cantor, New York
Mr. and Mrs. Moshe Castel, Tel Aviv
Mr. and Mrs. Nathan Cummings, New York
Harold Diamond, New York
Trude Dothan, Jerusalem
Dr. and Mrs. Henry Fogelman, Stamford, Connecticut
Nechemia Glezer, New York
Seth Glickenhaus, New York
Mrs. Adolph Gottlieb, New York
Mr. and Mrs. Chaim Gross, New York
Dr. Morton Hecht, La Jolla, California
Josef Herman, London
Mr. and Mrs. H. Lawrence Herring, New York
Marcel Janco, Tel Aviv
Mr. and Mrs. Joseph Kahn, New York
Luise Kaish, New York
Mrs. Corrine Kovarsky, Los Angeles
A. J. Lax, Kent, England
Richard Levitt, Des Moines
Yulla Lipchitz and Lolya Lipchitz, New York
The Albert A. List Family, New York
Mrs. Adele Lozowick, Milburn, New Jersey
Lee Lozowick, Parsippany, New Jersey
Sigmund Menkes, Riverdale, New York
Mr. and Mrs. Melvin Miller, Chesnut Hill, Massachusetts
Abraham Ofek, Jerusalem
Harold Paris, Oakland, California
Mr. and Mrs. Perry R. Pease, New York
Siegfried Poppe, Hamburg
Mr. and Mrs. Jack I. Poses, New York
Dr. Frank M. Purnell, New York
Bracha and Yitzhack Rager, Mitzpeh Ramon, Israel
Nathan Rapoport, New York
Mr. and Mrs. Raphael Recanati, New York
Charles H. Renthal, New York
Mr. and Mrs. Jack Resnick, New York
Mr. and Mrs. Yosel Rosensaft, New York
Mr. and Mrs. Harold J. Ruttenberg, Pittsburgh and Jerusalem
George A. Schneider, New York
Mr. and Mrs. Jacob Schulman, Gloversville, New York
Der Senator für Wissenschaft und Kunst, Berlin
I. Silman, Jerusalem
Raphael Soyer, New York
Mrs. Otto L. Spaeth, New York

Mr. and Mrs. Herman Spertus, Glencoe, Illinois
Mr. and Mrs. Jack L. Stein, Los Angeles
Igael Tumarkin, New York
Mrs. Samuel Weiner, New York
Clinton Wilder, New York
The Zorach Children, Brooklyn
Jacques Zucker, New York

Art Gallery of Ontario, Toronto
The Art Institute of Chicago
Associação Museu Lasar Segall, São Paulo
Department of Art, Brown University, Providence
The Ein Harod Art Museum, Israel
The Fogg Art Museum, Harvard University, Cambridge
The Solomon R. Guggenheim Museum, New York
The Hirshhorn Museum and Sculpture Garden, Smithsonian Institution, Washington, D.C.
The Israel Museum, Jerusalem
The Jewish Museum, New York
The Jewish Theological Seminary of America, New York
Kunstmuseum, Düsseldorf
Leeds City Art Galleries, England
Los Angeles County Museum of Art
The Metropolitan Museum of Art, New York
Museum of Art, Carnegie Institute, Pittsburgh
Museum of Art, University of Iowa, Iowa City
Museum of Art, The University of Oklahoma, Norman
The Museum of Denmark's Fight for Freedom, Copenhagen
The Museum of Modern Art, New York
National Museum, Warsaw
Newark Museum of Art
Park Avenue Synagogue, New York
Philadelphia Museum of Art
The Phillips Collection, Washington, D.C.
Städelsches Kunstinstitut und Städtische Galerie, Frankfurt
Stedelijk Museum, Amsterdam
The Tel Aviv Museum of Art
The Temple Museum of Religious and Ceremonial Art, Cleveland
Walker Art Center, Minneapolis
Whitney Museum of American Art, New York

Ben Uri Art Gallery, London
El Al Israel Airlines, New York
Fischer Fine Art Ltd., London
Forum Gallery, New York
Allan Frumkin Gallery, New York
Galerie Sumers, New York
Gimpel Fils Ltd., London
Kennedy Galleries, Inc., New York
Kraushaar Galleries, New York
Rosenfeld Art Gallery, Tel Aviv

Preface

Acknowledgements

What is the Jewish Experience? Has it been expressed in the visual arts? There may not be explicit answers to these questions but The Jewish Museum has chosen to respond regardless of the controversial nature of the questions asked.

The Museum has brought together a selection of works of art which visually link historical events, cultural themes, as well as the phenomenon of Jewish survival.

Jewish Experience in the Art of the Twentieth Century deals with values and themes which often give credibility to the concept of "Jewishness". Ambiguity in defining Jewish Experience raises numerous possibilities in the selection and juxtaposition of the works in this exhibition. The inclusion of examples without particular Jewish content, or abstract art (even those containing Jewish themes) may arouse controversy. Yet Jewish artists have been drawn into the mainstream of twentieth century art. Some will regard this participation as representing alienation from their Jewish heritage—others will regard it as an affirmation. The Jewish Museum believes that this is an historical phenomenon worthy of documentation.

We have attempted to portray a generalized Jewish Experience and have discovered that the complexity of the task is almost beyond definition. Thus the impact will vary depending upon the knowledge, personal values, and cultural heritage which each individual brings to the exhibition.

Joy G. Ungerleider
Director

I wish to thank the many museums, galleries, and private collectors without whose cooperation in finding and lending works, this exhibition would not have been possible.

I would like to thank Stephanie Barron for administrating the exhibition and for editing the catalogue.

My thanks to Susan T. Goodman, Curator of The Jewish Museum for coordinating the various efforts related to the exhibition. To Victoria Zelin for helping with details of the show. To Cindy Berkow and Gertrude Winograd for gathering the works. To Irit Miller of Haifa University and Paulette Jellinek who assisted with research. Thanks also to Tina Ben-Israel, Susan Gill, Theresa Greenfield, Stacey Miller, Caryl Walker Podet, Sarene Shanus, and Susan Vosk. Special thanks to Professor Moshe Barash of Hebrew University for sharing his ideas on the subject with me and Eduard Roditi for providing valuable advice. My appreciation to Professor David Noel Freedman. I am thankful to the supporters of The Jewish Museum Painting Conservation Workshop: H. Lawrence Herring and Jacob Schulman. I am pleased to acknowledge the Ministry of Education and Culture of Israel for help in transporting the works from Israel. My gratitude to Francis Ehrenberg, David Spilke, Jacob Schulman, and Corinne Kovarsky for generous contributions toward the exhibition catalogue and poster. My appreciation to Vera List, Dr. and Mrs. Frank Elevitch, and Mr. and Mrs. Phillip Kirkeby for making possible the inclusion of Harold Paris' environment *Kaddish for the Little Children*.

Avram Kampf
Curator of the Exhibition

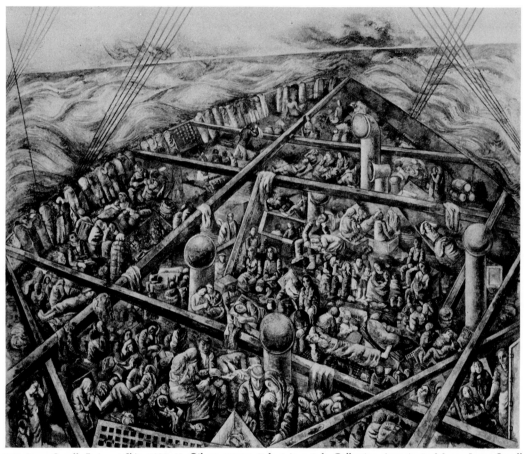

213. Lasar Segall. *Emigrant Ship*. 1939–41. Oil on canvas. 7 ft. 6 in. x 9 ft. Collection Associação Museu Lasar Segall, São Paulo, Brazil.

Jewish Experience in the Art of the Twentieth Century

Avram Kampf

The work of art does not fit into any of the conceptual categories which the rational mind constructs. It explodes them.

The work of art cannot be tamed into a social or personal document without imparing its essential character—integrating impulse, feeling, and thought and acting as a nodal point of formalized energy, shaping personal, historical and cultural motifs into an autonomous, self-sustaining world.

On the other hand, the work of art can never be completely grasped without sensing and bringing to consciousness the multitude of personal elements, cultural aspects, and historical relations that it contains.

There is a need to affirm that the tendency in the visual arts to regard works as autonomous esthetic objects only denies these essential truths. By disregarding their intricate historical context and seeing only formal qualities we diminish them. The art object is the vortex of individual and cultural experience. It is of its own time and transcends it. It is form and content, illusion and reality, affirmation and deception, conviction and play, sensual and spiritual.

One could choose a large number of works produced by Jewish artists and create an esthetically impressive exhibition by showing what they have done in the 20th century. One could even claim that whatever filters through a Jewish mind can be termed "Jewish Experience". To define the exhibition in this way would have made an extremely complicated issue simple, perhaps far too simple to be true.

Such an exhibition would at best show the wide participation and activity of Jewish artists in the 20th century in all art movements, but would have been sectarian without interpreting and clarifying the major and unique experiences which have marked the life of Jewish individuals and communities in this century. Experience is a continuous process of the living organism interacting with aspects of the world in which it lives. Experience means observing, encountering, and undergoing. It is feeling, sensing, thinking, and remembering. It means enduring situations and conditions, and it means changing. When many encounter or undergo similar conditions we may talk about shared or collective experiences, even though each person reacts in his own way to a common situation. As one scans the 20th century landscape of art one discerns salient features of the Jewish collective experience, which are only too familiar to those who have been alive in this century.

There have been the large migrations from East to West, from close-knit communities to a strange atomized world. There was a meeting with the culture, ideas, and art of the West. There are the problems arising out of the struggle to survive, to live, to assert, to act, and interact. There is a need to strike roots in a new environment, to adapt, assimilate, and yet to preserve one's identity. There are tensions between tradition and innovation, the options which life offers, and the decisions it forces on us. There are roads which are travelled, roads which part, cross and meet again. There are new beginnings, new landscapes, new cities, new planting, new work. There is a reconstruction and an affirmation, a losing and finding, which is echoed in the work of artists, whether born in America or Lithuania, whether setting up their easels in São Paulo or London, whether coming as immigrants to Israel or settling in Paris or New York, whether open, or closed to religious thought and feeling, or merely indifferent.

That this century has been one of continuous upheaval is known best by those who lived through it as observers, participants, victims, or survivors. There were the trials of the First World War, the period between the Wars, the catastrophe designated as the Holocaust with its trains and the death camps of the Second World War, the survivors wandering across Europe, sailing the seas, endlessly seeking new homes. There has been the continuous struggle for Israel, its building and defense, the encounter with the Biblical landscape, and the rebirth of an ancient language. That interaction between man and the world, which we call experience, produces friction and fissures in the individual and the collective, stirs emotions and ideas, and leaves the traces which we attempt to discover in 20th century works of art.

This exhibition defines itself by focusing on the Jewish background, concerns, or motifs which feed into the creation of the works. There has been a strong claim that modern art is largely built on the narrow esthetic precedents of other works of art, and that its formal problems grow out of older formal problems. This emphasis on formal invention and innovation has diminished the value of content. Not only has there been a tendency to devalue or deny the literal, the pre-artistic, the experiential sources of life which continuously nourish art; we have thereby been induced to overlook the relations, loyalties, and tensions between the artist, his background, his culture, sources and concerns. This exhibition rests squarely on life experiences collectively shared, intensified, interpreted and transformed by the artist. The exhibition is not assembled to illustrate or document Jewish history in the 20th century, nor is it an exhibition only of Jewish artists. This exhibition does not attempt to tell a story or demonstrate the existence of Jewish art. No exhibition could do that.[1] It is Jewish experience in the *Art* of the 20th century that concerns us. The exhibition refracts, however faintly, the Jewish experience by assembling works scattered in different places in a communal context. It thereby re-establishes the social matrix to which they originally were related, and out of which they emerged.

This theme, which controls the selection and arrangement of the exhibition, provides us with an original insight into 20th century works of art not hitherto assembled or studied as a group.

Works of art, however, do not fall neatly into any preconceived categories. Sometimes they only touch or hint at the experience which was their source; often they refer to it more directly. Occasionally the work has transformed experience so that it seems to extend beyond the boundaries of the exhibition. Our categories and comments should be seen as limited interpretations, having a bearing on particular historical data, not as restricting or confining the meaning or significance of the work of art. The classifications and groupings are intended to be ontological or metaphysical in nature, binding artists' reaction to events which may have occured far apart in time and place. Thus, immigration or new planting may refer to the different waves of immigration and new beginnings in England or the United States, or in Israel, at the turn of the century, in the forties, or currently. Our themes should be seen as points on an axis along which we gather 20th century works of art.

This exhibition makes no claim to completeness, either in the categories it proposes, or in the works of art or artists which were chosen. Nevertheless, for those who are interested in seeing contemporary works relating to the Jewish experience, and for those who have been impressed by the persistence of Jewish motifs in modern art, this exhibition offers a unique opportunity.

The exhibition *Jewish Experience in the Art of the Twentieth Century* comprises roughly the timespan between the painting of Samuel Hirszenberg, *Funeral of the Zadik*, and Ben Shahn, *Identity* (Nos. **92, 218**). Hirszenberg's dark and starkly dramatic picture painted about 1905 in Lodz, Poland, gives us the sense of a compact, cohesive community carrying its leader to rest. Like a bark tossed upon the waves of a restless sea, the coffin is carried on the shoulders, the hands, the intense emotions of the mourners. The artist, whether participant or observer, represents death as an intensely felt loss, as a traumatic event. The long horizontal composition, the overcast sky, the black coffin

92. Samuel Hirszenberg. *Funeral of the Zadik*. 1905. Oil on canvas. 30 x 81 in. Collection The Jewish Museum, New York.

218. Ben Shahn. *Identity*. 1968. Mixed media on paper. 40 x 27½ in. Lent by Kennedy Galleries, Inc., New York.

and the mass of darkly-clad mourners pressing forward, straining and stretching their arms in their effort to touch the coffin, convey an intensely communal and religious sentiment. In Ben Shahn's work *Identity*, hands stretch, tortured and grasping at nothing as if searching for purpose, for selfhood or identity, as its title implies. It can be seen as a picture of the modern post-emancipation era conveying a desperate quest for belonging and community. Hillel's saying, inscribed in Hebrew on the top of the canvas, "If I am not for myself, who is, and if I am only for myself, who am I, and if not now, when?" impressed the artist to a point that he seems to offer it as a piece of ancient wisdom, a golden mean between self-reliance and community orientation, and as a potent posture for contemporary man.

During the period between these two works the old East European Jewish community underwent a total transformation. It gave birth to the various Jewish national movements and at the same time was eroded by various social and historical processes: enlightenment, modernity, and assimilation which acted as solvents; and by the enormous destruction of the Second World War. The process of enlightenment was an important element in the dissolution of the traditional faith structure of the Jewish community, whether doubt was stirred through

contact with the world of learning from the outside or whether it arose from inner sources.

Mauricy Minkowsky's work *"He cast a look and was hurt"* (Hatzitz Ve'Hanifgah) (No. 168 is an early twentieth century version of a theme which preoccupied Leonard Baskin in his woodcut *The Four Mystics* (No. **30**, p. 44). In Minkowsky's version the accent is on the fearful moment of discovery of the forbidden book in the synagogue which could be Maimonides' *Guide to the Perplexed* or the *Zohar*, the Kabalistic *Book of Splendour* or any other book which was considered a threat to established faith. Baskin's woodcut *The Four Mystics* refers to an earlier second century encounter between representatives of the culture of ancient Judaism and mystic syncretic tendencies of the Greco-Roman world. The wise men were the Rabbis Ben Azzai, Ben Zoma, Elisha Ben Avuyah, and Akiva, who entered the *Pardess*, the garden of esoteric knowledge. According to the Talmud, Ben Azzai cast a look and died, Ben Zoma lost his mind, and Elisha Ben Avuyah lost his faith and left the fold; only Akiva came out of the garden with his faith intact.

The enlightenment period which generally marks the end of the Middle Ages came late for the Jewish community in Eastern Europe. It gathered force in the latter part of the 19th century, and its conflicts became manifest in social and religious life, leaving their imprint on the art and literature of the early 20th century.

Marc Chagall's picture *Calvary* illuminates in its composition, in its manifest and latent content, in its iconography and its symbolic gestures, much of the tension and conflict which enlightenment and the processes behind it brought into the Jewish community (see illustration). It points to the gap between the generations which enlightenment created and which drove artists and intellectuals beyond the Pale. In *Calvary* we face the ethereal figure of the pale blue child mounted on a pole as if he were being crucified, against the dark expanse of green color. Curved lines appear, disappear and reappear in the canvas as they converge on the child. The child is bemoaned by a tall bearded man with a torn sleeve and a small woman in a green dress decorated with little flowers. Both are firmly grounded in the red soil. A colorful river separates the red soil in the lower part of the picture from its vast green background. Palms and cactuses are on the other side of the river. A boy passes by in a winged boat with a sail which is the color of the blue sky, and an old man on the far right carries a ladder.

The appearance of the crucified child as early as 1912 is worth noting. It is a result of Chagall's migration to the West and the re-evaluation of the attitude of Jewish artists and men of letters towards the figure of Christ. Like many of the younger generation around the turn

Marc Chagall. *Calvary*. 1912. Oil on canvas. 68¾ x 75¾ in. Collection The Museum of Modern Art, New York. Acquired through the Lillie P. Bliss Bequest.

of the century, Chagall was powerfully attracted by the light which shone from the West. Its science, technology, and art were a magnet. They strove to cross the river or climb the fence which physically or symbolically encircled many of the Jewish towns and separated them from the rest of the world. They strove to break out of the confines of the ghetto and explore the world beyond the river, which might have meant Moscow, St. Petersburg, more often Berlin, Munich, London, New York, or Paris. To some it meant the Holy Land. In any case—cold, dark oppressive Russia was to be left for a brighter, sunnier climate. Parents saw in this process a threat to community stability and continuity. They saw their children leaving the traditional faith and mourned the loss. The children saw the process as a move upward and outward into a new and hopeful realm. Some Yiddish and Hebrew poems of this period express this yearning. They portray Christ, venerated by the outside world as a brother, a fellow-artist, a performer of miracles. For Chagall he will become the symbol of Jewish martyrdom.

At the beginning of the century the figure of Christ became an object of sympathetic contemplation as a new relationship emerged conditioned by historical insight and enlightenment; artists dealt in a secular way with ideas hitherto repressed or forbidden. Christ is addressed by the Hebrew poet who had emancipated himself as a brother who will in the future return to his people, wrapped in the traditional prayer shawl. The Yiddish and Hebrew poet Uri Zvi Greenberg writes:

. . . What happened to Jesus our
brother crucified
On several poles exiled in the world
Is it true that thousands of bells
   From thousands of towers ring
   For him
Has he sheaves on his head
and does he expose his

nakedness to the wind
To the rain
To the heat
To the lips of the people so
    that they can kiss him?

. . . he hangs there
on poles by day,
on stones by night
and no one saves him . . .

. . . he hangs in the middle of the world
and looks out to the end of all times
deep is his longing
he will return with a prayer shawl
around his shoulder
On the day of redemption
at the end of time
and the crown, which was removed
On his holy head . . .[2]
    [translated from the Hebrew]

But it was the Hebrew poet, Saul Tchernichovsky, who broke sharply with tradition when he expressed the attraction which enlightenment generated for art. Writing in Odessa in 1899 he exhibited a totally new attitude toward the West and its art. In a poem, he addresses Apollo:

. . . I come to thee and bow before thine
    image,
Thine image–symbol of the light in life:
I prostrate myself to the exalted and the
    good,
To things of high estate upon the earth,
To all majestic in creation's bounds,
To all the highest mysteries of art; . . .[3]
    [translated from the Hebrew]

Russian national art, which had its center in Moscow and which formed the basis of modern Russian art, reacted against neoclassicism and the artistic hegemony of the St. Petersburg Academy of Art by basing itself largely on the Russian peasant and his folk art. Likewise, Jewish artists who, before the Revolution were attracted to various branches of the Jewish national movement mainly for cultural and esthetic rather than political reasons, were concerned with the creation of a national art, based on Jewish book illuminations, gravestone carvings, and synagogue decorations which were all considered folk art. Among the artists who participated in this trend were Nathan Altman, Issachar Ryback, Marc Chagall, Boris Aronson, and El Lissitsky (Nos. 11, 19, 64, **148, 152,** 205, 207).

Lissitsky was refused entrance into the St. Petersburg Academy of Art because he was a Jew, and went on to Darmstadt, Germany to study architecture. After matriculating in 1912 Lissitsky travelled extensively in Europe visiting France, Italy, Switzerland and the Balkan countries. He returned to Russia shortly after World War I had broken out. In 1916, Lissitsky,

19. Boris Aronson. *Untitled.* n.d. Woodcut on paper, 14 x 11 in. Lent by the artist, Grandview, New York.

152. El Lissitsky. *Lion* (from Synagogue of Mohilev wall painting). 1918. Watercolor and charcoal. 9 x 9½ in. Collection Boris Aronson, Grandview, New York.

along with Ryback, explored the wooden synagogues along the Dnieper, marvelling especially at the architecture and ornamentation of the famous Synagogue of Mohilev of the eighteenth century. He copied several of these wall decorations (Nos. **152,** 153).

Ryback's painting *The Old Synagogue* (No. **205**) probably derives from impressions gathered during those ramblings through the countryside with Lissitsky. Between 1911 and 1914, the ethnographer and playwright S. An-ski headed

11

205. Issachar Ryback. *The Old Synagogue*. 1917. Oil on canvas. 57½ x 38⅛ in. Collection The Tel Aviv Museum of Art.

an ethnographic expedition in the towns of the Jewish Pale and collected material of Jewish folkart, folklore and demonology which he later used in his writing of the mystic play, *The Dybbuk*.

The research in Jewish folk art was not felt to be in contradiction to the various abstract tendencies of modern art which Lissitsky had encountered first hand in European art centers, and which were eagerly cultivated among the avant-garde painters in Moscow. The naive character of folk art was seen as a significant source of modern art. Hence the pursuit of folk art afforded the Jewish avant-garde artist the opportunity to combine the expression of Jewish national sentiment and the tendencies of modern art.

Lissitsky, in his various illustrations of Yiddish books such as the *Chad Gadya* story (No. **148**) used modern abstract motifs in the lettering and illustrations and linked them with aspects of primitive folk arts.[4] The same tendencies are found in the woodcuts of Boris Aronson (No. **19**), in Nathan Altman's work on Jewish ornament, and in Marc Chagall's illustrations of the stories of Peretz and Der Nister (The Hidden One) which are closely related to the Hebrew alphabet. The impact of Der Nister on Chagall must still be assessed. Der Nister was a student of Kabalistic lore and succeeded in his songs, fairy tales, and dream images in combining European and Hebraic elements.

The Old Synagogue and the *Succoth Still Life* by Ryback (Nos. **205**, **206**) both reflect an interest in

148. El Lissitsky. Study for cover from *Chad Gadya*. 1917. Brush, gouache, pen and ink, traces of pencil. 11 x 9 in. Collection The Museum of Modern Art, New York.

cultivating Jewish folk art, while embracing the abstract tendencies of modern art. This group of artists, who often exhibited together in their attempt to promote contemporary Jewish art, was encouraged by collectors such as Kagan Shabshay who actually planned for a Jewish

Museum in Moscow before the 1917 Revolution, and by the establishment of the Moscow Kamerny State Yiddish Theatre and the Hebrew Habimah Theatre after the October Revolution. These theaters were under the strong artistic influence and direction of Konstantin Stanislavsky and his pupil Evgenii Vakhtangov. They provided a meeting ground for the interaction of all avant-garde movements in drama, dance, music, literature, and painting. Musicians, painters, actors and directors worked consciously for the development of a national Jewish culture and style. They all rode the wave of revolutionary enthusiasm. They were finally free after centuries of oppression by the Czars. At that point everything seemed possible. As Jews they were now full-fledged citizens. As avant-garde artists they were recognized spokesmen of their age. Altman, who, like Chagall and Lissitsky had spent some time in Paris, designed the modern sets for *Uriel D'acosta* in the Yiddish State Theatre and for Habimah's most famous play, *The Dybbuk*. Altman was appointed head of the Fine Arts Committee of St. Petersburg and was responsible for the celebration of the first anniversary of the Revolution. There he designed the decorations of the great square in front of the Winter Palace and staged the famous "happening", The Storming of the Winter Palace. The Revolutionary government appointed Chagall Commissar of Art of Vitebsk and the head of its Fine Arts School. Lissitsky was appointed professor of design, and under the influence of Malevitch created the first of the series *Proun* (No. 151).[5]

Encouraged by the liberal policy of Lunatcharsky, the first Minister of Culture of the Soviet Union, the artistic activity continued intensively for several years. In the Yiddish Theatre, Chagall designed the sets for three one act plays of Sholom Aleichem for Alexander Granovsky and Solomon Michoels. His designs opened the way to a deeper understanding of Sholom Aleichem and contributed to the unique achievements of the Yiddish Theatre. Chagall's "influence was visible not only in the stage sets, costumes, and make-up technique, but even in the gestures of the actors . . . The actors found in the grotesque stylization of European gesture and the exaggeration of the Jewish, as well as in folklore, what they needed to express their idea of the Jewish character. In many respects they came close to the conception expressed in Chagall's forms."[6]

64. Marc Chagall. *Over Vitebsk.* 1914. Oil on paper mounted on canvas. 27½ x 35¼ in. Collection Art Gallery of Ontario, Toronto. Gift of Sam and Ayala Zacks, 1970.

Chagall's *Green Violinist* is a late version of *Music* which together with *Dance, Drama* and *Literature* were parts of a large set of murals Chagall painted for the Yiddish Theatre in Moscow. The paintings *Purim* and *Feast of the Tabernacles* (Nos. 66, 59) are based on sketches Chagall originally prepared for a Jewish secondary school, housed in the same edifice as the chief synagogue of St. Petersburg. In these and other paintings of the period Chagall, who had returned to Russia in 1914 after spending four years in Paris, perceived that the essence of Hasidism was remoteness from a life grounded in everyday reality. In Chagall's work we can see the awkwardness and enthusiasm of the Hasid, his lack of self-consciousness, his obliviousness to the here and now, his rhythm, posture, gesture, intimacy and charm, and the color and tone of Yiddish proverbs.

It was their distinctive lifestyle and attitude which Chagall grasped and rendered in pictorial form. Being a Jew was a way of life, a way of dressing, walking, talking, eating, fiddling, wrapping oneself in a prayer shawl, courting, kissing and loving. It was a way of working, arguing, smoking and dancing; it was the way one spread one's fingers or stuck one's hand out. There was something airy, unreal and unnatural about the figures he painted. They were homely and grotesque with their chickens, their goats and their cows, with their clocks and their fish. But whatever one could say about them they were also very funny, coarse but not vulgar, colorful and unpredictable, endowed with that vitality of oppressed people who feel that they are princes disguised as beggars and believe that in the world to come they will be kings and sit at the table of Almighty God. While Chagall's uniqueness is already evident in his early paintings and drawings, his stay in Paris during 1910–14 freed his latent power, provided him the tools of his craft, and gave definite direction to his art. His religious themes are marked by a certain folk–like quality rather than by intense emotion. He painted the Jews who were still living in an environment dominated by religious observance, manifest in custom and dress. It was a way of life, pervaded by religion, in marked contrast to the norms of religious behavior in the West (Nos. 60, **64, 70**).

An attitude of personal reverence and a tone of inner religiosity can be sensed in the etching

125. Jacob Kramer. *Day of Atonement.* 1919. Oil on canvas. 39¼ x 48⅛ in. Collection Leeds City Art Galleries, England.

Separation (*Havdalah*) by Herman Struck (No. 244), the two depictions of Friday evening by Isidore Kaufmann and Ben-Zion, and the Louis Lozowick painting *Lone Worshipper* (Nos. 114, 34, 156). There is primitive religious strength in Jacques Lipchitz's sculptures *Sacrifice* (No. 145) and *Prayer*. Walt Kuhn's sabbath bread is an object of profound reverence (No. 126). A sense of priestly domination and strong rejection is implied in *Figures with Upraised Arms* by Maryan S. Maryan (No. 161). Intense religious experience is conveyed in *Day of Atonement* by Jacob Kramer (No. **125**). This painting reflects the strong influence of Vorticism, a combination of Cubist and Futurist forms, which emerged in England under the influence of Wyndham Lewis. By repetition of the figures, wrapped in their prayer shawls, the artist achieves the unique and intense rhythm of a congregation standing in silent prayer. A more festive mood of religious prayer comes to the fore in the canvases of Hyman Bloom, Moshe Castel, and in the painting *Cohanim Blessing* by Sigmund Menkes (Nos. **47**, **57**, 164). Ernst Troeltsch had observed that genuine religious feeling is to be found only among the lower classes; Karl Marx said "Religion . . . is the heart of the world in a heartless world". Marvin Cherney's *Man with Torah* (No. 73) is remarkable for the unconventional say in which the man grasps the Torah; it represents a burden, it represents a child.

The *Synagogue* by Abraham Ofek (No. 178) conveys something of the unconditional religious belief of the worshippers. The congregants have a grotesque expression. Religious service is a cementing force without which the group cannot exist. Menkes' painting *The Uplifting of the Torah* (No. **166**) painted in Paris in 1928, carries the mark of a highly personal statement and takes us back to the experience of the artist's childhood. Intense tribal feeling emanates from the canvas in which the Torah scroll is lifted and unrolled and the figures around the scroll exhibit a spontaneous and unconditional devotion. There is a great deal of movement as people press forward in their desire to come close and touch it. The centrality of the Torah is underlined by the circular composition of the figures around the scroll, which guards the people as they guard the scroll. The concept of the *Brit*, a passionate belief in the covenant between God and His people, embodied in the sacred Torah, is expressed as the intimate experience of suffering and yearning people pressing towards the light of the Torah. There is no differentiation here between priest and layman, only the Torah itself is crowned. The boy in the foreground (who bears a distinct resemblance to the artist) stretches his hands in amazement and completes the circle around the Torah. His youthful features stand in marked contrast to the bearded faces of the men.

In Max Weber's *Adoration of the Moon* (No.

47. Hyman Bloom. *The Synagogue*. 1940. Oil on canvas. 65¼ x 46¾ in. Collection The Museum of Modern Art, New York. Acquired through the Lillie P. Bliss Bequest, 1943.

253. Max Weber. *The Talmudists*. 1934. Oil on canvas. 21 x 26 in. Collection The Jewish Museum, New York.

166. Sigmund Menkes. *The Uplifting of the Torah.* 1928. Oil on canvas. 86 x 65 in. Private collection.

251) a primitive visionary mood prevails and in *The Talmudists* (No. **253**) the focus of religious activities has been shifted from prayer to the study of the Torah. Plain people engage seriously in the most rational and educational aspects of Jewish communal prayer, the study of the Torah and its commentaries. They are gathered in a vaulted room, a man-made cave which has become a world of study, in which the artist explores various attitudes and processes. There are those who study in solitude, who meditate and quietly absorb what they have read, those who express surprise at certain passages, those who argue with others about fine points. Weber's distortions are not to be seen as caricature, they arise out of keen observation and subtle discernment and preference, out of great admiration and strong poetic impulse. Weber must have watched those people in Bialystock, whence he came as a child to America, or in New York on the Lower East Side. The painting is an homage to the house of learning. "What are they", remarked Philo already in the 1st century C.E., "but schools of wisdom and temperance, and justice and piety and holiness and even virtue, by which human and divine things are appreciated and placed upon a proper footing."

It is not difficult to sense in this long-standing tradition of learning the cornerstone of discipline, rationality and reverence for the work of the mind, a training ground for those who even after they left this particular kind of house of learning made their mark in the sciences, literature and art of the century. The painting by Ben-Zion *Jewish Bookseller* (No. 35) portrays a man who is also something of a scholar, and Moses Soyer depicts a thoughtful lover of books (No. 236). David Aronson's *Teacher and Student I* (No. 22) and *Dispute II* (No. 20) deal with the transmission of knowledge and the examination of truth and justice or the interaction of both themes, which engaged the artist for many years.

There is a Jewish experience of vigorous participation in the intellectual and artistic work of the modern world, the root of which can be seen in the house of learning. The elements of passionate abstraction in the works of El Lissitsky, Naum Gabo, Antoine Pevsner, Adolph Gottlieb, Mark Rothko and Barnett Newman are derived, as we shall see, from this background, although their work cannot be reduced to their Jewish heritage.

From the second decade of the 20th century to the time of the conquest of France by Germany in 1940, Paris became the home of a great number of Jewish artists, painters and sculptors, who came mainly from Eastern Europe and spent the best years of their creative lives there. Among the artists who arrived early in this period were Alfred Aberdam, Marc Chagall,

Jiri Kars, Moshe Kiesling, Michael Kiköine, Pinkus Krémènge, Jacques Lipchitz, Mané-Katz, Amedeo Modigliani, Chana Orloff, and Chaim Soutine. In the twenties Max Band, Sigmund Menkes, Abraham Mintchine, Rueven Rubin and others went to Paris. Most of these artists were in their early twenties, all of them were unmarried, and none had independent means (Nos. 1, 169, 171, 228, **231**).

Those who arrived from the East, and they were by far the great majority, felt the transition to be an especially sharp one. Writers speak about the shock of Paris. There was the experience of being free, of being able to sit on a bench without the policeman chasing you away.[7] There was the sheer physical beauty of the city and the spirit of friendship, acceptance and equality in the artistic community. There were the museums which represented the art of all ages, and there was the vigor of contemporary French painting. When the Jewish painters arrived, the Fauvist wave was receding and Cubism was re-evaluating the foundations on which Western painting had based itself since Giotto. In this atmosphere those who had studied in the East disregarded quickly what they had been taught and re-examined their ideas about art in the light of the new esthetic which emerged in the studios and in free discussions which artists engaged in wherever they met.

It has been noted by Waldemar George that the stereotyped view of the Jewish artist, who comes from a small, backward but sympathetic village of ghetto to Paris to make his mark there, has to be discarded. While some of the artists came from the most squalid, ignorant and unloving circumstances, others came from large modern cities, from well-to-do and assimilated families. But the intensity of artistic activity in Paris and the conditions of modern art, the stress on originality, individuality and invention made it possible for each artist to find his own road to fulfillment. Whatever his perception, whatever his temperament, whether mystical or rational, expressionist or romantic, he could expect a sympathetic hearing within the artist community; and the value of his activity would be enhanced by the activities of others.[8]

Doubtless, the fact that there was no classical tradition behind them, that they were strangers and wanderers made it easier for them to join the movement of modern art and commit themselves to various avant-garde positions. Jewish artists, because of their common language and common background tended to meet frequently. Some historians speak about an enclave of Jewish artists, others about a Jewish School of Paris. The gathering of a relatively large number of Jewish artists in Paris is a fact of 20th century art and of Jewish social and cultural history.

Chagall, who came to Paris in 1910, has been identified largely by the way in which he

231. Chaim Soutine. *Landscape at Céret.* 1919. Oil on canvas. 28¼ x 20¾ in. Collection Mr. and Mrs. Nathan Cummings, New York.

33. Max Beckmann. *Synagogue.* 1919. Oil on canvas. 35½ x 55⅛ in. Collection Städelsches Kunstinstitut und Städtische Galerie, Frankfurt. Acquired 1972 by gifts of citizens of Frankfurt and by means of the City of Frankfurt.

combined Jewish Hasidic and folkloristic motifs with elements of 20th century French painting. We have already touched on his work in Russia after his return there in 1914. In retrospect, it was not Chagall, but rather Soutine who became the leading figure among the Jewish artists in Paris. The distinctness of Soutine's vision, his absolute modernity, the echo he evoked in others, and the very wide influence he exerted on the modern art movement made him a formidable figure.

Soutine seems to have had a greater impact than any other artist on the Jewish painters of his generation. His personality and style reflected the thinking, the feeling and mode of living of less well-known painters like Michael Kiköine, Pinkus Krémègne, Jacques Chapiro, David Seifert and others. While Chagall's mysticism is that of the Hasidim, the mystical element in Soutine's work is of an intimate personal nature, it is experience itself, the dread of existence, closer to Kierkegaard than to the Rabbi of Nemirov or Peretz. Chagall cast a nostalgic look and produced his work out of reverence and love for the past: a vision so personal and lyrical could not be shared by others.

There is not a single painting by Soutine which we can identify as being Jewish in subject matter, there is no iconographical symbol which is even remotely related to Jewish historical memory, no painting which is a tribute to his past, his family, or his childhood. The absence of any artistic reference to the Hebraic tradition or the events of his own early life is rather striking. Other artists found in both areas rich sources and natural avenues for artistic expression. Soutine is silent on this point and from what we know of him we may assume that repression plays a large role. Nevertheless, he is seen by many of his critics and fellow artists as a very Jewish, un–French, painter.

The work of Soutine seems wild, unpremeditated, lacking logic, construction or plan. Chaos and turmoil emanate from his canvases. In his landscapes, houses seem to slide down the hill, trees turn and twist as if caught by the whirlwind; children flee from the tempest. His still lifes consist of dead fowl, slaughtered oxen, and flowers which glow and curl as they grow twisted and tortured out of the vase. The colors, sensual, visceral, with finely nuanced brush strokes combine to form fleshy patches, quiver as if they would never come to rest. There is a clear preoccupation with the materiality of physical substance, with primordial and decaying matter. The portraits are deformed and their faces prematurely old, awry and painfully distorted, their hands clasped, their bodies stiff or leaning from their chairs in an attitude of discomfort, self-containment, or despair. He paints cooks, porters, page–boys, men and women without name or status (Nos. 228, 229, 230, **231, 232**, p. 63).

Here is no fairyland of Chagall, none of the latter's humor or childhood dreams. The canvases are a wild storm, a tempest whipped by fear and fury, by the nervousness and the anxiety of the hunted and persecuted. They are extremely sensuous, imbued with a deep spiritual and metaphysical quality, colors are resonant, played fiercely against each other, somber reds against deep blacks and abysmal blues, contrasts are sharp, values masterfully controlled. The work contains the poetry and violence of the victim, the stranger, the outcast, the creature lost in a world he has not made. It is the work of an artist who yearns for relief and redemption in the very act and process of painting, in the immediate impulsive and spontaneous response to what he sees and feels, who finds refuge in creating agitated textures, in spreading pigment with fingers and brushes over old shabby canvases. His work emanates from a life experience which did not know of planning, of stability, of harmony or of a confident look into the future.

He is representative of the artists who came from the Ghetto to Paris. Eli Fauré, who knew Soutine, was among the first to call attention to the artist's ethnic background, in which he saw the key to an understanding of Soutine's painting. He seemed not to be quite sure if he were an Asian, a Tartar, or a Jew:

> This face of an Asian whose forehead is covered by his hair, who is driven by the force which compels the magician who looks for the stars. He is less a Jew than a Tartar if you look only at his physical type, but if you know his habits he is a Tartar just like a Jew. He goes after an ever-changing horizon, and his nightly escapes are an escape from himself and his quest to find at some crossroad, stability, some point of rest which does not exist . . . From where does he have the ability to paint, so seldom seen in the East and almost unknown with Jews? . . . Perhaps the suddenness of the freedom gave birth to this desire, I don't know. We only can say all or partly a Jew, a great painter who came from the Ghetto of Minsk.[9]
> [translated from the French]

To French art critics, Soutine's work seemed utterly perplexing. Maurice Raynal, writing in 1928, reacted to it with a mixture of admiration and scorn; Soutine's art seemed to him:

> . . . an expression of a kind of Jewish mysticism through appallingly violent detonations of color. His work is a pictorial cataclysm, comparable, in its exasperated vision, to the reckless frenzies of martyrs and heroes.[10]

And speaking about Soutine's landscapes and figures he considers them:

. . . an ebullition of an elementary Jewish rigorous Talmud, has kicked over the Tables of the Law, liberating an unbridled temperament and indulging at last in an orgy of criticism, destruction and reconstruction of nature—cursing the while and cursing very copiously, its Creator.[11]

Waldemar George refers to Soutine's background:

The curse which rests on the painter rests on his race, it decided the whole psychic life of the artist. It leads his hand and his brush . . . Formal art has nothing to do with this kind of creation, which is all release and elevation . . . Soutine does not revolt against Raphael or the Academic art. He does not know it. He is free, desperately free, totally free . . . The most emphatic expression of the Jewish genius is his mobility . . .[12]

[translated from the French]

Maurice Tuchman suggests that Soutine's preoccupation with animals and food was a symbolic violation of Jewish law and his stress on the importance of concretely conceived objects, a reaction to the visual prohibitions of Jewish doctrine deeply honored in the "Shtetl".[13]

While the intrinsic Jewishness of Soutine's work will remain a matter of controversy and opinion, it is perhaps interesting to note that Israeli art critics, owing to a feeling of kinship and identification with the mood of Soutine's canvases, have responded to him as one in whose pictures "all the terrible events of our generation" were felt.[14]

Soutine was the eleventh son of a poor mender in Smilovitchi. His father was not a skilled craftsman, "but only put patches on clothes, he never made a suit".[15] Soutine exhibited an unacceptable penchant for art at a very early age. His older brothers wanted desperately "to drive out the Dybbuk of painting"[16] from Soutine. They treated him so badly that he would run away from home for days at a time.

These and other well–documented, turbulent events in Soutine's childhood would go far to explain some persistent features of Soutine's work: his relationship to his home, to people and the world. Yet we know too little about the laws of genius and how it fulfills its function with energies of desperation, to indulge in psychoanalytic speculation. We know very little about his student days in Vilna, except that he was actively interested in the theater, where he displayed a strong dramatic capability. While he had very little contact in Paris except with the Russian Jews, he befriended Seroya, a man versed in Spinoza and the Kabala, and Chana Orloff and her son who was a biologist. Soutine generalized from his own experience to include all men and the whole world. His energies mobilized the spirit of rebellion toward the past, the ghetto; he insisted on the primacy of self, of his own total experience, which was to him the highest form of sensation. Thus, Soutine emerges as an artist–hero, the forger of a new style and a new vision, toward which many other Jewish artists in Paris gravitated. Soutine, who had torn himself from his surroundings and his past, created an art, which was filled with nervousness, anxiety and fear—the life experience of others who were less articulate in the medium. His work was believed to mirror the situation in which they and all European Jewry found themselves in the period between the two World Wars. It was seen to prefigure the Holocaust.

There was hardly an artist in Europe who was not affected by World War II. Jewish artists became refugees and went into hiding. Many were sent to the concentration camps, and a large number died there.

By 1919 one observes signs of foreboding in the painting *Synagogue* by the German Expressionist Max Beckmann (No. **33**). The purple walls of the building, the oblique stance of the houses and the people on the square, the evil-looking cat, various hostile inscriptions on billboards and advertisements, and the dim light coming through the windows, create an eerie threatening mood. Beckmann sensed the violence in the atmosphere and what the future was to bring.

Chagall's *Study for Solitude* of 1933, in which a Jew with Torah and calf sit forlorn on the roadside, suggests the dire events to come. He may have felt the approaching catastrophe as early as the twenties when he started working on *The Falling Angel,* a work which he continued during the thirties and only completed in 1947. *White Crucifixion* of 1938 (No. **72**) was the first of a series in which the artist reacted to the mounting crisis in Europe. The figure of Christ is central and accentuated by the shaft of light cutting diagonally across the picture. Franz Meyer has commented that this is by no means a Christian representation.[17] The artist reminds us of Christ's Jewishness by integrating him into contemporary Jewish history. Christ's loin cloth with two black stripes resembles the traditional Jewish prayer shawl. Neither is he portrayed as God's Son, who by taking upon himself the suffering of the world redeems it. Meyer writes:

Here instead, though all the suffering of the world is mirrored in the crucifixion, suffering remains man's lasting fate and is not abolished by Christ's death. So Chagall's Christ figure lacks the Christian concept of salvation. For all his holiness he is by no means divine.[18]

The world around the central figure is in a state of upheaval. Everything is in motion and tilted, except for the Menorah at the foot of the cross,

72. Marc Chagall. *White Crucifixion*. 1938. Oil on canvas. 61 x 55 in. Collection The Art Institute of Chicago. Gift of Alfred S. Alschuler.

which is the only solidly vertical object in the composition. Its opalescent circle of light is balanced by the halo around the head of Christ. A Jew in the lower left grasps the Torah and turns his head back to the synagogue, which is on fire. Chairs are overturned in the lower right, and a Torah scroll thrown on the ground is burning. The flames spread to the bottom of the ladder, which leans against the cross. A Jew escapes with a sack on his shoulder. In the left corner a man weeps and another carries a sign that once read in German, "I am a Jew." In the upper left an armed mob invades the village, houses tumble, and people escape in a boat. Nearby, instead of the traditional angelic mourners, common Jewish figures grieve.

Through these and other paintings, Chagall expressed, by means of symbols deeply embedded in the art of the Christian West, the tragic events of the Holocaust and some aspects of its profound religious and historical dimensions.

Jankel Adler's fate as a Jewish painter in Germany was sealed when the Nazis came to power. He had established himself as a significant force in German painting of the twenties, and participated in every important Expressionist show. Many of his works were lost or destroyed, and after he was forced to flee Germany in 1933, he wandered restlessly through many lands—France, Poland, Russia, the

8. Jankel Adler. *Two Rabbis*. 1942. Oil on canvas. 33⅞ x 44⅛ in. Collection The Museum of Modern Art, New York. Gift of Sam Salz, 1949.

Balkans, Spain—until he joined the Free Polish Army. After he was discharged, he settled in Glasgow, where he exerted a major influence on post-war British painting.

In Adler's painting *Two Rabbis* (No. **8**), the heavy-set figures confront us with monumental seriousness as they plead for mercy for their people. The urgency of their plea is concealed behind their silent appearance—the tight lips, the small penetrating eyes, the carefully combed beard and hair, create a tense enigmatic image which tends toward abstraction. In their pleading, one senses the denial of the plea, the deafness and lack of response. The rabbis become icon-like representations of wisdom, rationality and human dignity. All formal elements—composition, color, and texture—serve as the projection of an idea, rather than merely providing visual representation. The word "Misercor" [dia] (pity), written on the tiny scroll the rabbis carry, seems to be addressed to no one in particular. It is an essential part of their own humanity.

Adler differed from most Eastern Jewish artists in that he did not go to Paris, but made his home in Düsseldorf. There he experienced the strong influence of German Expressionism. His persistent interest in the technique of painting—exploration of new textures—derives largely from his studies with Gustav Wiethuechter, at the School of Arts and Crafts in Barmen. He also was influenced by Klee and Picasso. With Klee he had close personal contact, for in 1931 they both taught at the Düsseldorf Staatliche Kunstakademie and had adjoining studios.

Some critics have drawn comparisons between the nature of Soutine's apocalyptic vision and the Holocaust. Others have remarked upon the affinity between the grave seriousness of Jankel Adler's figures, his firmly constructed compositions, the deep resonant colors of his paintings, and the strength and severity of Jewish orthodox religion in which he was raised. Some see in Adler's paintings a blending of the mathematical clarity of the Talmud, with the mysticism of the Kabala (No. 4). Many of the portraits he painted are of members of his family, and often he used traditional Jewish themes or introduced Hebrew letters into his work.[19]

A powerful sense of identification with the Jewish people emanates from many of Adler's canvases, a point to which Else Lasker Schüler refers in a poem she dedicated to him:

> *Weiht er doch jedes Bildnis das er malte,*
> *Mit dichterischer, grosser Harfenschrift*
> *Seinem jungen Gotte Zebaoth.*[20]

[He dedicates every one of the pictures that he paints with a large poetic harplike inscription to his young God, Zebaoth.]

Concerning Adler's *Two Orphans* (No. 7), his friend, the painter Josef Herman, relates:

> In 1942, the Red Cross transmitted to me a message that my whole family in Poland had perished. I was terribly distressed. One day, Jankel Adler appeared at my studio and brought me this picture he had painted as a gift. There are two orphans in the picture; after a while I understood that one was me and the other he himself.[21]

Artists born in the late twenties, became the youths vicitimized by the Nazi terror. Some were inmates of concentration camps; others were troubled by what they knew and feared.

Yosl Bergner was born in the shadow of the Holocaust. An apocalyptic mood permeates the objects that haunt the artist (Nos. 36, 37, **39**, 40). Various household articles appear in his canvases—graters, pots and pans, spice boxes, tea kettles, chairs, doors, and closets. They fly through the air, over the sea, like birds and leaves; they are carried by drafts of air to a distant shore, walk on the desert sand, lie prostrate on the seashore, their destination unknown. The postures of these objects remind us of human beings: like them they bend, stretch or recline. The graters especially assume human features. They are nailed to the pole, wrapped in loincloths, or pried apart by powerful tools. Blue and silver-grey, they have been torn from their surroundings, are homeless and displaced. They are worn, dented, perforated and broken, battered from use, tinny and hard. They are personal and collective objects, secular and sacred, invested with a particular warmth, smell, touch, and quality of home. They bring back indelible memories of childhood, of place, of play, and of family.

The symbols of a destroyed community, of an inexplicably twisted life, of escaping, wandering, searching, dominate the paintings of Yosl Bergner. Born in Vienna, he spent his youth in Australia and came to Israel via Canada, America, England, and France. Distant, ever-shifting and crisscrossing frames of reference have made the irrational commonplace. The experience of the strange and the surreal in

39. Yosl Bergner. *Empty Room.* 1966. Oil on canvas. 36 x 36 in. Collection Mr. and Mrs. Harold J. Ruttenberg, Pittsburgh and Jerusalem.

the existence of man and community became at an early stage the norm of the artist's vision.

Erich Brauer's painting, *Persecution of the Jewish People* (No. **52**), is a series of seven paintings. Born in 1929, Brauer was sent at age 13 to a Nazi workcamp. There he saw more than his share of pain and degradation, but in a wondrous way, he overcame those difficult years, and integrated and balanced their bitter memories with early childhood experiences, which play an important part in his work. When in 1945, the Russian tanks crossed the canal of the Danube, he fled from the workcamp. "My garden was the burning city of Vienna,"[22] he wrote later. He enrolled in the Vienna Academy of Fine Arts while the building was still smoking.

Brauer was very much the product of Viennese circumstances. As an adult he draws strength from vivid childhood memories. There were colorful beggars, cripples, strange men and women and street gangs. There was his father, the cobbler, who used to hum Yiddish and Hasidic songs while repairing shoes. All these turned his childhood into a delightful, enchanting memory.

Brauer's work is strongly influenced by the Viennese school of Fantastic Realism, which established itself after the Second World War as a distinct movement on the continent, and of which he is a leading figure. He sees himself an heir of the Viennese Secession tradition, and extended its concept of total art into his own life, which he transformed into a "work of art." Brauer turned his canvases into a paradise where childhood fantasies dwell side by side with the vision and daydreams of adults. Human figures, plants, and insects are metamorphosed into a colorful transparent, legendary world, bathed in light, with groups of people interlaced boisterously in a Breughel–like atmosphere.

Many of Fritz Hundertwasser's paintings derive from childhood experience. In *House with Yellow Smoke* (No. **95**, back cover) green houses are surrounded by sharply pointed bright yellow–green fences, placed in an intensely brilliant red area. There is a mark of a footstep in the red. Yellow, red–streaked smoke issues from the chimneys. It is similar to another painting, *Jew's House in Austria* where the houses too seem to drown in a sea of blood.

Hundertwasser, the son of a Jewish mother and a German father who died shortly after his birth, found himself in a most precarious legal situation. Eleven years old when the Nazis marched into Vienna, he became the protector of his Jewish mother, grandmother, and aunt who had enrolled him in the Hitler Youth Organization for his safety. When the boy came home from his activities, he would enter the door of his apartment on which a yellow star was fastened by law. When at midnight the SS made their usual surprise inspections, the boy was prepared to fend off the SS officers for the sake of his family. As the knocks at the door were heard, he would quickly slip into his brown Hitler uniform and meet the SS men at the door, wearing the several medals that his father, a German officer, had won in the First World War. He thus "proved" to them his pure Aryan descent. This arrangement was successful on a number of occasions, but once there came a time when it failed. As usual, there were knocks in the middle of the night, but these were very light. He repeated the well–rehearsed performance, but it turned out that the people at the door were not SS officers but Jewish Auxiliary Police. They took his aunt and grandmother, and he never saw them again (No. 94).[23] In 1943, Hundertwasser made his first conscious crayon drawing from nature. In the same year, sixty–nine of his Jewish maternal relatives were deported to Eastern Europe, and killed. Hundertwasser remembers hiding with his mother in a trench in 1945 during the last days before Vienna was conquered by the Russians. He was terribly fearful that he would be denounced as a Jew to the SS and be killed.

While the spiral labyrinth and the decorative aspect of Hundertwasser's work can be related to a tradition stemming from Gustav Klimt, Egon Schiele, and the Viennese Secession, they cannot be seen as strictly formal motifs. His spirals are quite different from those of Klimt. Less regular, they often change form, thin and swell, become square and change colors. It would be rash to restrict the appearance of this theme to the traumatic events of the War. The artist's experience must have been a contributing factor in the selection of this preferred form, which clearly satisfied deep psychological needs. He himself thought of the spiral "as a fortress that I have constructed for myself in an unknown territory . . . a bulwark for myself against my environment."[24] Indeed, in the theory of military defense, the connection between fortress and spiral is still very much alive. The purposeful irregularities of labyrinthine structure, and the long narrow winding paths are designed to confuse the attacker and thus create a certain advantage for the defender. The artistic form of the spiral–like labyrinth was always the carrier of important symbolic values. The one–way direction of the path that leads from the outside toward the center creates for the eye a beautiful pattern that is easy to comprehend, but hard to follow; it symbolizes man's capacity to progress toward his goal, without doubting or turning back. There is a compelling force about the obsessive repetitiousness of a spiral pattern. It is a sensuous expression of the inescapability of fate and necessity, an archetypal image that follows sinuous incomprehensible lines to a center, where Theseus fights the fateful battle with the Minotaur to gain his freedom. The center is the end of a perilous journey; it is a sacred place where salvation lies. Once we start a spiral, we abandon the possibility of returning for a fresh start or a new beginning. Its form is a perfect metaphor for an infinite journey.

Today, Hundertwasser and Brauer continue to paint a paradise of dream enchanted memories. Their art is beautiful to behold, decorative and life-enhancing. Form and color have transformed their experiences. Brauer lives in Vienna, from which he frequently escapes to the exotic Orient. Hundertwasser built a boat—a new country—where he escapes from the problems of men, a floating island where he rules sovereign.

Maryan S. Maryan was deported with his father to Auschwitz, and spent his childhood in the most infamous of the death camps. His leg had been badly injured and had to be amputated. After liberation he spent his youth in German camps for displaced persons, working as a stage designer for the Jewish theaters organized among the inmates. He had lost his family; there was nothing to which to return. He went to Israel, but could not find a home, and continued on to Paris and New York. Maryan carries the Holocaust within him, and it is manifest in everything he paints: inmates of camps, prisoners with striped uniforms, inquisitors, victims, jailers, sharp–clawed cats, horned lions, slaughtered lambs with a sharp–toothed predatory look, as if they were both hunters and hunted. He paints priests who raise their arms in a gesture of benediction, but their faces are merciless (No. 161). He creates strange human beings with donkeys' ears and long tongues sticking out in defiance and dejection, dying bulls with colorful banderillos piercing their necks, medieval knights with shining armor, open–mouthed without eyes (No. **163**). His paintings are filled with butterflies with dog-heads, interlacing worms, monsters and eyeless machines which resemble human beings. He paints condemned people with pointed hats, men with wheels

163. Maryan S. Maryan. *Personage, Man with Donkey Ears.* 1962. Oil on canvas. 50 x 50 in. Lent by Allan Frumkin Gallery, New York.

screwed to their hands, legs and chests, imprisoned in narrow cells. Maryan's work is by no means literary; he makes use of the values of abstract designs. Although he generalizes from what he himself has undergone, we know only too well the sources of his images. Compared with his experience, nightmares are Utopia. That he could give them form testifies to his strength as a person and as an artist.

The theme of the Holocaust is central in Samuel Bak's work. Like Brauer, Hundertwasser and Maryan, he too is a child of the Holocaust. He spent early years under German occupation in the Vilna Ghetto. His father was shot a few days before he and his mother escaped the burning quarter. He was one of only 150 survivors among 80,000 Jews of that city famous for its Jewish learning and academic tradition. Yet, even while he was wandering through the

27. Samuel Bak. *The Traveller.* 1972. (triptych). Oil on canvas. Left: 39½ x 32 in. Center: 39½ x 39½ in. Right: 39½ x 32 in. Collection Victor Barnett, New York.

52. Erich Brauer. *Persecution of the Jewish People* (detail). 1973-4. Oil on canvas. 40 x 32 in. Lent by the artist, Vienna.

170. Abraham Mintchine. *Self Portrait.* 1926. Oil on canvas. 31⅞ x 21 in. Collection The Israel Museum, Jerusalem.

occupation zone from camp to camp toward Palestine, his mother saw to it that he had whatever instruction in drawing was possible, as well as the materials needed to develop the talent that he had displayed very early. Later he wrote, "I grew up without a permanent address, without a father and without God."

Even as a child he felt the utter absurdity of finding any moral logic in the events surrounding him. Samuel Bak became a painter philosopher. His impressions were so dreadful that they could not be told as they were, so he fell back on symbolic language. In the painting, *The Family* (No. 23), he pays homage to the people, dead and alive, to whom he feels related—from his great-grandfather, the dignified inventor whose features remind us of Leonardo da Vinci, to his soldier friends still in battle dress with whom he fought in Israel's wars. The picture is an assembly of faces and figures like an old-fashioned group portrait. The figures are set against a sky darkened by smoke and glowing with the reflections of distant fires. These are the people he remembers with various degrees of intensity, which he expressed by showing them alive, embalmed, silhouetted in relief, petrified, or as incomplete monuments. They had little idea of the fate that awaited them.

Having matured as an abstract painter, Bak turned suddenly, under the influence of a protracted stay in Italy, to the tradition of the Renaissance. Today he blends his own experiences with images drawn from specific art historical sources. Bak thereby implies a criticism of "achievements" of the twentieth century—its technology and its art. *Father and Son* could be called "The Sacrifice of Isaac," although there are hints of the story of Daedalus and Icarus, a sacrifice for the sake of mechanical invention and progress. In several of his paintings, man seems trapped by technology. Metal wings, wires, and mechanical paraphernalia are attached to man and angel, making their attempt to rise and reach the sky absurd and ridiculous (No. 24).

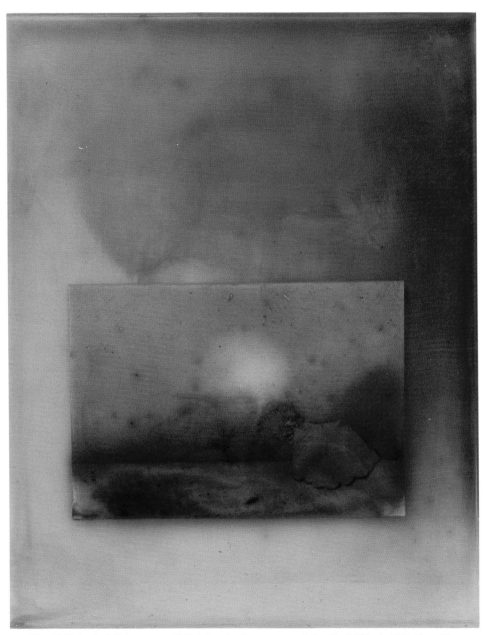

183. Harold Paris. *Soul Series 1975—All that Remains* (in memory of the Six Million). 1975. Cast silicone and colorants. 12½ x 10 in. Lent by the artist, Oakland, California.

Harold Paris, born in 1928, experienced the Holocaust when, as an American soldier—an illustrator for *Stars and Stripes,* he was among the first to enter the Buchenwald camp after the Allied Forces discovered it. The son of an actor of the Yiddish Art Theater, Paris has always been preoccupied with performance and ritual, death and immortality, the sacred and the numinous. He brings to his work a sense of drama, a mastery of new materials, new processes and their combination in multimedia art. Wonderment, blackness, and the occult are part of his private mythology, which is attuned to hidden combinations that he discovers in places, events, Hebrew letters, poetry, reminiscences, and ideas. The theme of life and death is never far from him. He has made a series of biomorphic bronze and plastic sculptures, which he called *Chai (Life),* and is known to have put one of them in a coffin and buried it in an elaborate ceremony. He has created ceramic walls called *Mems,* after the Hebrew letter Mem, because they are the initials for the Hebrew words, *mal'ak hammawet* the angel of death, Moloch (an ancient tyrannical Semitic deity), and Malach (angel), as well as the capital letters of the names of Majorca, Madrid, and Munich—three cities in which he stayed in 1950.

The Holocaust, ever on his mind, includes all that happened in Europe during the War, and all that happened in Vietnam and America during the 1960s. In his notes, Paris envisioned a room that he would make and seal so that no one could enter and see his dream—the sculpture he had placed inside (No. 181). This room was a "Kaddish," a "Homage to the past, to wonderment and loneliness . . .

> What does it look like?
> Like the inside of a) my soul.
> Who can see it?
> Only the blind with two small
>   children
> Where does it come from—
>   the wail of the shofar
>   the 3,000 years
>   and a scream in Vietnam . . .[25]

This was a

> Kaddish for all the 'lost' in my—your life, all that cannot be again . . . This huge black room, this ineffable statement—black, black and inside is all the wonder I can evolve—all the love I project and summon forth . . . .
> . . . What is it—this Kaddish—this refutation? It is a long, long voyage into my past—the war, my childhood, the constant searching and seeking. A black solemn box, solemn and brooding and with it all that I know (and do not know, but sense and feel.) White, white forms with heat and cold imbedded—gutting these irresolute shapes. To make this huge chamber and to stand

mute, unknowing, severed, torn, bleeding within. Before it a small mound to gaze and stare and ponder at these never to enter walls. No one may ever see this room to wonder at and to know. The blind can be witness to this—tell us—What do you see? All of the blood and pain of time sits within—truly for you it is sealed and a seal upon my life and mind. No door, no entrance and no one to enter . . .[26]

He pays homage to the souls of artists dead and alive, to whom he feels close, to the souls of events and objects that move him. The soul, that which endures, that which ascends and descends according to a Hebrew song that he must have heard in his father's house, he enshrines in a sensuous, intimate, luminous, translucent and dematerialized form.

The *Souls* are slabs of silicon gel, in which objects are embedded and into which delicate colors, organic, inorganic, and phosphorescent have been fused in the process of solidifying. They have the quivery resilience of human flesh and are analogous to the frailty and vulnerability of human life. *Moment in M,* and *All that Remains* are voyages into realms that move and concern the artist. (Nos. 182, **183**).

The events in Europe cut deep into the consciousness of artists everywhere. Alfred Aberdam, who was hiding in Paris during the German occupation, painted *Deportation* (No. 1), a somber, dark picture of men, women and children, gathered silently in the street in an atmosphere charged with apprehension. Mordecai Ardon, who had fled to Jerusalem, painted *Train of Numbers* (No. 16), which, with its sharply edged lines and numbers slashed across the landscape and the sky, evokes the rhythm of freight trains speeding the tattooed victims to their death.

The physical torture and brutal degradation of inmates in the camps is evoked in the works of Edward Kienholz, Mauricio Lasansky, Rico Lebrun, Olly Ritterband, and Lasar Segall. Pablo Picasso's *Charnel House* is based on the atrocities of Buchenwald (Nos. 128, 115, 197, 210).

Jack Levine's *Warsaw Ghetto* (No. 138), based on a widely-known German photograph, depicts women and children with raised hands being marched through the streets of Warsaw.

Sigmund Menkes, a painter of joyousness of life, turns to a sombre palette in his paintings of the Holocaust—*The Trial* (No. 165) and *Uprising of Ghetto Warsaw* (No. **167**).

Kurt Seligman expresses the mood of war in *Sabbath Phantoms-Mythomania* (No. 216), where ghost-like figures walk in barren landscapes.

Abraham Rattner, in *Ezekiel's Valley of the Dried Bones* (No. 190), paints a tangled, chaotic abstract canvas, influenced by photographs from concentration camps.

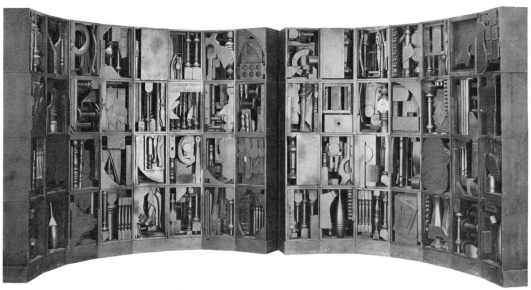

175. Louise Nevelson. *Homage to Six Million I.* 1964. Painted wood. 108 x 216 in. Collection Department of Art, Brown University, Providence, Rhode Island. Gift of The Albert A. List Family Collection.

43. Naftali Bezem. *Binding of Isaac (Akeda)* (detail). 1968. Oil on canvas. 35⅜ x 51¼ in. Lent by the artist, Jerusalem.

Luise Kaish went to Dachau in order to sketch the doors of the ovens in preparation for *Holocaust* (No. 109).

Homage to Six Million I, (No. **175**) by Louise Nevelson envelopes the spectator in a phantom–like black structure created from stacked boxes which are filled with familiar objects—legs of chairs and tables, abstract shapes resembling discs, violins, organ pipes, all vestiges of former dwellings.

There often appear the traditional themes of the Akeda; The Binding of Isaac and Jacob Wrestling with the Angel. The Binding of Isaac appears as an illustration by Ephraim Moses Lilien (No. 142), an artist who works in the Art Nouveau tradition, and later in the work of Israeli artists: Naftali Bezem (No. **43**), Schraga

167. Sigmund Menkes. *Uprising of Ghetto Warsaw.* 1943. Oil on canvas. 41 x 25 in. Lent by the artist, Riverdale, New York.

29

199. Reuven Rubin. *Arab Fisherman.* 1928. Oil on canvas. 30 x 24 in. Collection Mr. and Mrs. Harold J. Ruttenberg, Pittsburgh and Jerusalem.

Weil, Mordecai Ardon and others. The Binding of Isaac occupies a central place in Jewish religious and social history. It is a trial of faith imposed on Abraham, the founding father of the Jewish religion. Abraham's willingness to heed God's request has traditionally been held as the highest model of fidelity. The struggle for survival has brought the reality of the ancient myth of the Akeda into the consciousness of contemporary Jews. Jacob wrestling with the angel *(Genesis* 32:25) tests the limits of human

strength in the struggle for survival. By an act of will and faith, man transcends himself. Max Band (No. 28), Elbert Weinberg (No. 256), and Nathan Rapoport (No. 189) found that Biblical motifs gave meaning to contemporary trials.

Art follows life like a shadow. History forces its themes on artists. Images of ships on high seas, packed with homeless persons with no friendly shore in sight emerge from experiences immediately following World War II. Mitchell

Siporin reacts in a moving work, *Endless Voyage* (No. **227**), which depicts the plight of the refugees who find no refuge but are determined to reach the land of Israel.

Lasar Segall, who established himself as a painter in Brazil, draws on his own experience there, stemming from his first voyage in 1912. A mature painter from Vilna, he studied in Germany, and was intimately connected with German Expressionism when he sailed from Hamburg. Spending four weeks on board ship between sea and sky, among the human cargo emigrating to Brazil, he stored impressions to which he returned in 1947, when he created the large canvases which dealt with refugees floating aimlessly, unable to land (Nos. 212, **213**, frontispiece). The canvases are painted in muted greys and ochre-toned passengers overcrowd the deck. In *Exodus* (No. 214), Segall spiritualizes the painting by erasing the boundaries of the ship, but hints at them through the composition of the figures on deck.

Jacques Lipchitz, whose art is rooted strongly in the Biblical and Jewish tradition, and who has been extremely sensitive to the mood of his times, created a menorah sculpture, *Exodus*

(now lost), whose stem and arms formed the mast and sails of a ship from which people hung. His works *Mother and Child* (two versions), and *Arrival* have their source in these events. In *Mother and Child* from 1930, the child is carried by a kneeling and groaning mother, and in the later tragic *Mother and Child* of 1941–1945, the mother raises her mutilated arms and the child clings to her. Both echo the mood of helplessness and desperation of this period.

The Yiddish theater, which had its historical source in the "Purimspielers", accompanied Jewish immigrants from Eastern Europe, providing entertainment. The spirit of Yiddish theater included the audience, which was an active and interested participant in the drama. This is evident in the drawing and painting of the Jewish theater by David Bomberg. The drawing *Jewish Theatre* (No. 50) was done in 1913 when Bomberg graduated from the Slade School of Art in London where he studied together with other painters who were children of East European Jewish refugees. Mark Gertler, Jacob Kramer, and the poet–painter Isaac Rosenberg all attended the school. Bomberg's works are

120. Yehoshua Kovarsky. *Temple Above the Moon.* 1958. Oil on canvas. 40 x 50 in. Collection Mr. and Mrs. Jack L. Stein, Los Angeles.

227. Mitchell Siporin. *Endless Voyage.* 1946. Oil on canvas. 34½ x 39⅜ in. Collection Museum of Art, University of Iowa, Iowa City.

probably based on visits to the Pavilion Theatre at Whitechapel, where *Hamlet* was performed in Yiddish. It was the only place in London where the plays of Gogol, Chekhov, Strindberg and Tolstoy were performed. They could only be understood by Yiddish–speaking people. Bomberg grew up in an Orthodox family in London's East End when it was a teeming immigrant section similar to New York's East Side. There Yiddish was spoken; literature, theater, and social issues were debated with great intensity and intellectual vigor; and new ideas of the world were eagerly examined and absorbed.

Jewish Theater shows a strong search for expressive interlocking forms and differing postures and attitudes of engaged spectators. In the painting, *Ghetto Theatre* of 1920, (No. **48**) Bomberg visibly moves away from naturalism and tradition. He strips irrelevant matter from his subjects, and by means of Cubist–influenced language, moves toward bold simplification of forms without losing interest in the essential characteristics that mark a popular audience and their involvement with the stage. Bomberg's

work was among the first in London to show marked influence of the new artistic developments in Paris. *Mud–Bath* and *Vision of Ezekiel* are early indications of his interest in Jewish subject matter, to which he often returned.

Wherever Jewish immigrants from the East went, they brought attitudes they had formed in their homeland and ideas that agitated them. The inroads that enlightenment and modernism had made, their historically–conditioned alienation from manual work, and the continuing influence of the Biblical tradition, made them susceptible to the ferment of socialist ideas. The unsuccessful Russian Revolution of 1905 brought masses of Jewish workers imbued with various Socialist, Anarchist, Bundist, and Territorialist ideas to America, Socialist Zionists came not only to America, but also to Palestine. Wherever they went, they organized unions, educational and social facilities. Socialism became a dominant force in Jewish intellectual and communal life, filling the void of fading religious beliefs. Many of the artists in this exhibition

48. David Bomberg. *Ghetto Theatre.* 1920. Oil on canvas. 30 x 25 in. Lent by Ben Uri Art Gallery, London.

250. Abraham Walkowitz. *East Side Crowd.* 1903. Ink on paper. 10 x 7 in. Collection Mr. and Mrs. H. Lawrence Herring, New York.

were children when they came with their parents to America, or they were the children of immigrants.[27] They carried with them childhood impressions from Eastern Europe and the culture of their parents' homes. We find them active in the realist tradition of American art, in ascendancy at the beginning of the century under the impetus of Robert Henri and the Ash Can School, in subsidence after the Armory Show of 1913, and reappearing strongly during the Depression and the Work Projects Administration. We find them also among the pioneers of the modernist movement in America, first centered around Alfred Stieglitz' 291 Gallery, and then associated with the Abstract Expressionist painters in the creation of a new American art.[28]

America was different; everyone was an immigrant. For the artist, the situation was not unlike that in Russia immediately after the 1917 Revolution. Everything seemed possible. One could head the design department of the Congress of Industrial Organizations or paint the murals of a post office one day and design the ark of a synagogue or the windows for a church the next day. One could do stage designs for the Yiddish theater and for Broadway at the same time. During the twenties, there was an obscure club of writers and artists called the "Jewish Art Center". Among its founders were Abraham Walkowitz, Benjamin Kopman, and Jennings Tofel. Other members included Yiddish intellectuals, poets, writers and actors.[29] Their purpose was to encourage the creation of a distinct secular culture within a pluralistic

74. Jacob Epstein. *East Side People.* 1900-01. Chalk on paper. 26¼ x 23¼ in. Collection The Jewish Museum, New York. Gift of Karl Nathan.

85. William Gropper. *Tailor.* 1940. Oil on canvas.
21¼ x 26¼ in. Collection The Hirshhorn Museum and
Sculpture Garden, Smithsonian Institution,
Washington, D.C.

society. However, they failed to take into account
the dynamic nature both of American society and
of 20th century art.

In Eastern Europe, as we have seen, there
was a folk base in the art relevant to the Jewish
masses. Around 1900, Jewish intellectuals
became conscious of Jewish folk art and were
eager to explore it. It seemed then that conditions
were ripe to develop a Jewish national art. In the
United States, this folk culture dwindled
increasingly as it was absorbed into the stream of
general immigrant culture. Only the religious
aspect remained intact and retained some of its
visible particularity. Yet, the struggle for Israel,
memories of the parents' home, and mainly the
literature of the Bible and the Kabala continued
to stimulate many artists. Jewish neighborhoods
had an immigrant flavor. They were noisy and
compact; Yiddish was spoken; and Yiddish signs
and newspapers were widespread. The small
shops, the teeming neighborhoods, the familial

238. Raphael Soyer. *Artist's Parents.* 1932. Oil on canvas. 28 x 30 in. Lent by the artist, New York.

environment formed a distinct sub-culture, which many painters knew intimately. The vitality of the streets is rendered sometimes as a warm, human, colorful spectacle, in the romantic realism of Jerome Myers (No. 173); in the rigorously realistic drawing by the sculptor Jacob Epstein (No. **74**); in the crowds painted by Abraham Walkowitz (No. **250**). We see it too in the intimate surroundings of Jennings Tofel (No. 248), in the portraits of pressers by David Levine and William Gropper (Nos. 133, **85**), and in the early cityscapes by Raphael Soyer (Nos. 240, 242). There are traders with their stalls, peddlers, straphangers; men, women, and children interacting spontaneously in their strange colorful costumes. For the newcomers and artists, these were fields of curiosity and exploration.

Raphael Soyer's *Artist's Parents* (No. **238**) gives us some clues about the artist's father. He was a teacher of Hebrew literature and history in Russia, a *Maskil* ("Enlightened One") rooted in the Hebrew tradition and open to ideas of enlightenment and liberalism. He wrote tales for children and short stories and novelettes for adults in the style of Chekhov. A lover of art and music, he taught his sons to draw while still in Russia, where he decorated the cold and dreary walls of his home with postcard reproductions of Russian art in a fan-shaped design and spoke to his sons about Raphael, Rembrandt, and Michelangelo. His library included books by Tolstoy, Turgenev, Twain, and Dickens, which the children read in Russian. In the painting, the father has a powerfully developed head and a face lined with fine, sharp features and charged with intellectual energy. The man seems somewhat disoriented and worried; he supports his head with his hand. His thoughts are far away. In contrast, his mother places both hands on the table; she is centered on the here and now. The composition is reminiscent of *Absinthe Drinkers* by Edgar Degas, an artist whom Soyer greatly admired. *Dancing Lesson* (No. 239) is set in a middle-class Bronx apartment typical of the one to which the family moved following their arrival from Russia. Raphael Soyer describes the picture:

> It was a 20 x 40 canvas, which I called the *Dancing Lesson,* depicting our sister Rebbie teaching Moses to dance to the harmonica music of our youngest brother Israel, who was pictured sitting on the sofa with Avrohom and our grandmother. Near them, on a heavy rocker, sat Beyla with a Yiddish newspaper in her lap. On the floor was a flower-bordered rug. The blue wall was embellished by an enlarged framed photograph, popular in those days, of our grandparents. Beyla's rubber plant was in the corner.[30]

In their social awareness and the democratic impulses, Soyer's themes continue the tradition of the Ash Can School. The influence of John Sloan is particularly felt in his sympathy for people: transients, peddlers, derelicts, and office girls. His canvases are peopled with laundresses, dancers, dressmakers, poets, and pregnant women. His brother, Isaac Soyer, reveals the same sympathy for the unemployed (No. 235), while the portraits of Moses Soyer (No. 237) penetrate deeply into the character of his subject.

Louis Lozowick, in a self-portrait shows us the various cultural and professional phases of his development; he is guided in his art by his Socialist convictions. In *The Concrete Mixer* (No. **155**), men and machines interact harmoniously, serve each other, and even assume some similar features. In the lithographs and paintings of various American cityscapes (Nos. 154, 157), Lozowick expresses his faith in the powers of industrialization, and invests his images with the attributes of stark rationality, objectivity, repetition, precision and efficiency associated with the machine. These unique qualities of the machine are transferred to the towering architectural masses of American cities. Their simplified geometric forms are precise and somber, at once static and dynamic, and derive from the Futurist and Constructivist vocabulary of modernism. Abstraction here is not a flight into the private realms of imagination; rather it is harnessed to the dream and promise of a well-ordered industrial society. Formally, these pictures relate to the Cubist-Realism tendencies of Charles Sheeler and Joseph Stella which appear in American art during the twenties, and to Lozowick's interaction with the Russian Constructivists in Berlin in 1922.

In Jack Levine's *The Passing Scene* (No. **135**), there is an inkling of concern at being lost which is transmitted from the father to the son, and an expression of melancholy and fear appears in the eyes of the son. We are struck by the emaciated horse pulling its load, the insecure stride and anxious glance of the father. One senses it might not be just an ordinary street that Levine paints, but that the father moves symbolically into a no-man's land across dangerous territory. In this picture, we also note the sad-looking, overworked, emaciated white horse, which often appears in the canvases of Levine (No. 139). He carries his burden silently, like Bontsche Schweig, the suffering character of the Peretz story, or Rosenante, or the white Klatchke who may have jumped out of the pages of Don Quixote or of Mendele's story and wandered into the streets of 20th century Boston.

Jack Levine's *Tombstone Cutter* (No. 137) reflects the Holocaust in Europe. The man assumes the character of the carved material, as if the chisel he holds has cut deep furrows over his face, arms, body, and knees. The old man, an

135. Jack Levine. *The Passing Scene*. 1941. Oil on board. 48 x 29¾ in. Collection The Museum of Modern Art, New York. Purchase, 1942.

artisan, is at rest. The anatomy of his body, the mood of contemplation, the hanging lamp, and the ornamented tombstone accentuate the element of time. Photographs of an old Jewish cemetery or a tombstone store on New York's Lower East Side might have been used as models. The painting evokes thoughts about life and death, continuity and roots.

Jack Levine's *Planning Solomon's Temple* (No. 136) seems removed from the present—as if the artist had gone back far into his Jewish heritage. In actuality, the painting relates to the death of the artist's father, and it is also an unconscious reaction to the collapse of the WPA, which had at one time employed the artist and provided him with a sense of communtiy. As family and friends surrounded his father's coffin at the Boston Cemetery, Levine suddenly saw his father, once a poor shoemaker, as the head of the clan—the king of all Israel who was now robed royally with a prayer shawl before being lowered into the ground. In the painting, one of a series dealing with his father—who was called Reb Shlomo Hachacham (Rabbi Solomon the Wise), King Solomon unrolls the ground plan of the Temple, and King Hiram stands near him holding a trowel and a compass. Solomon is

crowned and dressed in oriental attire while King Hiram, with his workman-like dress looks more like the builder than the king. Hiram possesses the distinctive features of Jack Levine. By a subtle process of symbolic transformation, displacement and condensation, the painter who was out of work after the collapse of the WPA, isolated and mourning the passing of his father, sees his father now as the king who has risen from death, preparing a large program for public construction, and he sees himself employed again as a painter enjoying the prestige of a king.

The rejection of one's parents' tradition, which conflicts with the values of the environment, is revealed by Larry Rivers in *Bar Mitzvah Photograph Portrait* (No. 198). Joe Lasker in *Scissor Grinder* (No. 130) also points to sources of conflict. The large scissor and the Yiddish sign threaten the child leaning against the hydrant. In *Memo* (No. 129), the issue is clear. There is a portrait head of a Greek sculpture on the right, representing worldliness; an arm bound with phylacteries on the left is symbolic of the confining tradition of the home. The child must choose.

The variety of sources from which Ben Shahn draws in his painting, *Ram's Horn and Menorah, East Side Soap Box* (Nos. 222, **217**), and the portraits *Labori et Piquart, Georges Piquart* (Nos. 220, 221), point to the social and Jewish issues which concern Shahn. In particular, *Ram's Horn and Menorah* enables us to see the attempts to combine symbols of the Hebraic tradition and contemporary ideas of the equality of man and man's hope for redemption. In this sensitive and forceful statement Shahn has synthesized images born from the struggle of the working class with the iconography of religious motifs, pointing to their common ground in the words of the prophet (*Malachi* 2:10): "Have we not one father? Has not one God created us? Why do we deal treacherously every man against his brother to profane the covenant of our fathers?" The quotation in Hebrew calligraphy, which Shahn knew well, runs across the entire length of the painting. These lines appealed to an artist who had executed murals for the WPA and worked for the CIO. He painted it in preparation for a mosaic mural in the vestibule of Temple Oheb Shalom in Nashville. Yet, its elements had appeared earlier. Dominating the painting is the blue hand that emerges from the red flame and symbolizes the presence of God. The hand refers to God's creative power and intervention in the affairs of man. The figure sounding the shofar is wrapped in what seems to be a traditional prayer shawl. It is spiritualized by a severe distortion of the features and has a haunting ghost like quality due to the ash-grey overtones of his skin, and his enormous square pupiled eyes which stare at the spectator. The tension lines that surround the eyes are echoed in the many lines of the prayer shawl that envelopes his head, and in the detached, tense ceremonial position of the fingers that barely grasp the shofar. The men seem to be waiting for the great blast of the ram's horn. Waiting, as one of the conditions of human existence, is a theme that fascinated Shahn, and that has consciously been accepted by generations of Jews who elaborated it into a cultural force in their history. The powerful hand which emerges from the red flames of the Shekhinah pleads, demands, even threatens. It is at once a hand of compassion that "uplifts those who fall," and a warning raised against those who deal treacherously with their brothers.

The image of a disembodied hand had precedent in ancient Jewish art. It appears in the scenes of Abraham's Sacrifice in the ancient synagogues of Dura Europos and Beth Alpha. Ben Shahn's hand, however, is a worker's hand taken from the vocabulary of twentieth century Social Realism. It is interesting that Shahn, especially in his later periods, grounds his Socialist ideas in myth and religious thoughts. He constantly enriches his art through a combination of actuality and allegory. Deeply rooted in his consciousness were several significant religious experiences of his childhood while still in Lithuania. Early attitudes of skepticism that he developed did not lead to a lifelong hostility toward religious themes.[31] He seems later to have found in religion and its literature, sources of humanist thinking. *East Side Soap Box*, a scene that Shahn must have witnessed in his youth, documents the culture of Jewish workers, their social convictions, their organization, their leadership, and their own Jewish consciousness.

When one's perception is bent by the promises of a promised land, when the eye is not riveted to immediate needs and one carries a blueprint of an earthly paradise in one's pocket, the strife-torn land of Israel looks as quiet and peaceful as it does in the canvases of Reuven Rubin. His landscapes are serene: villages merging into gently sloping hills, donkeys loaded with fruit travel on winding roads (No. 200). His canvases are peopled with Hasidic Jews dancing in ecstasy, colorful Arab fishermen throwing out their nets or offering fish for sale (No. **199**, p. 30). Skinny black goats eat from the trees. The landscapes with their ancient olive trees, whose silver-leaved feathery branches grow toward a hazy and filmy sky seem legendary and Biblical Young women with long black braids and almond-shaped eyes carry the first fruits of the season or Sabbath bread toward home (No. 203). Boys carry flowers or play the flute. Window sills are filled with ripe pomegranates, and through the window a caravan of camels walks beside the sea.

Indeed, Rubin painted a promised land. His works are distinguished by a strong architectural sense and are filled with simplified forms, reminiscent of the innocence and naivete of Henri Rousseau.

217. Ben Shahn. *East Side Soap Box*. 1936. Gouache. 17½ x 11¼ in. Private collection.

Their bright colors reflect the artistic will of one who delights in forms appropriate to the simple pioneering society settling in Israel. The Biblical and midrashic imagination rule the canvas. The romantic nationalism, with its oriental and exotic overtones that emerged in Israel in the early twenties—largely under the influence of Reuven Rubin, was the first attempt to create a native Israeli art and to celebrate the hopes and values that brought idealistic people to the new country.

Rubin went to Palestine in 1912 at the age of 18, with the intention of studying art at the Bezalel School of Arts and Crafts—a school established with the support of the Zionist movement in 1906, under the leadership of the conservative sculptor, Boris Shatz. His decision to go there had been made long before:

From my early childhood I had dreamed of going to Palestine. It seems to me now that I always knew instinctively that that was the country where I would develop as a 'Jewish Artist.' By 'Jewish Artist' I don't mean a painter of Jewish subjects, but one whose roots are embedded in the soil of his own homeland, Zion—where the Bible lives naturally for him and where he feels in his rightful place and is spiritually at ease. I could not have been more than six years old when I began to feel and understand the call of the land of the Bible.[32]

Later he writes:

> How can one ever forget being eighteen years old, and coming for the first time to Jerusalem on a beautiful spring day to fulfill a dream? In the little Turkish train that brought me from Jaffa, I had my eyes glued to the window, gazing at the landscape and breathing in the air of Eretz Israel. I could hardly believe that it was I, Rivile, from the little town of Falticeni in the Carpathian mountains of Romania, who was actually in Palestine, travelling toward the hills of Judea. I was amazed to note that everything looked familiar to me; it seemed as if I knew every rock, every tree, the desert hills. As the train came to Jerusalem, I felt I was coming home.[33]

In order to understand a passion one has to be part of it. The romantic and nationalist mood can also be found in the paintings of veteran Israeli painters such as Israel Paldi, Nahum Gutman, and Moshe Castel. They revolted against the academic teachers whom Boris Shatz had brought from Eastern Europe to the Bezalel School, and who had not come under the influence of the new modernism. Rubin spent a year at Bezalel, then left in disappointment over the poor instruction and the philosophy that guided the school. In the following seven years, he returned to Rumania, studied in France, went to Italy and New York, and absorbed various artistic influences. He was particularly impressed by Ferdinand Hodler's work; he returned to Israel in 1922 to settle. He continued painting in a serene and joyous mood. His works are marked by an archaic quality and an absence of conflict—they are a celebration of wholesomeness and fulfillment.

Under the impact of the School of Paris, Israeli painters like Josef Zaritsky, Avigdor Stematsky, Yehezkiel Streichman, and their followers come close to creating pure abstract compositions. Their early sun-drenched landscapes and cityscapes dissolve in colorful compositions of expressive, sensitive, and dynamic brush strokes. Their styles, removed from any mystical or idealistic interpretation, disregard the world of appearances and move toward painting for painting's sake. Romantic idealism continued well into the thirties, when more artists arrived in Israel, some of whom had studied in Germany and Austria. Palestine was then a land of hope and vision; people felt reborn and formed a new society.

Johanon Simon studied with Max Beckmann in Frankfurt and spent several years in France with a group of young artists who gathered around André Derain. In 1934, he worked with Diego Rivera in New York, Tired of decadent aspects of art and life in the West, he went to Israel in 1936 and joined a kibbutz in which he spent seventeen years. He believed then in the possibility of being a member of the collective society, a worker and an artist. Like other members of the kibbutz, he tended bees, worked as a carpenter, drove a tractor, and irrigated the orange groves. Soon he found himself decorating the dining room of the kibbutz for holidays, and later painting canvases that celebrated the self-governing young men and women workers who had created new social forms of living.

In Simon's paintings the composition, the strong architecture, intuitive tendency towards verticality, monumentality and sculptural forms, show traces of Léger, Beckmann, Derain, and Rivera. Simon's art is not lyrical, romantic, or exotic, nor does it succumb to a sterile classicism or the dogmas of Social Realism. There is a *Kunstwollen,* a will to art, which draws on the sources of Israeli experience and creates the colors and forms that evoke the desert, heat, and the collective will. He renders the hard and resolute outlook of the heroic days of the kibbutz and reflects the values which this society placed on simplicity of living, hard physical labor, on cooperation and mutual help, on communal rather than private property, new forms of leisure, childrearing, education, and cultural developments (Nos. 223, 224, 225, **226**).

The kibbutz was the most concrete manifestation of the change in attitude toward physical labor in twentieth century Jewish history. There, labor was seen as an essential aspect of the rebirth of the individual and the community, healing the distortion of exile, by turning the social, economic pyramid back on its base. Physical labor was given a quasi–religious status.

This attitude toward manual labor was not

208. Shalom Seba. *Shearing of Sheep.* 1947. Oil on perspex. 18⅞ x 24¾ in. Collection The Tel Aviv Museum of Art.

confined to the kibbutz. Contrary to accepted belief, many of the Jewish immigrants in America were artisans who swelled the needle and building trades.[34] Louis Lozowick in *The Concrete Mixer* (No. **155**), David Levine in *The Pressers* (No. 132), William Gropper in *Tailor* (No. **85**), Isaac Soyer in *Employment Agency* (No. 235), and Raphael Soyer in *Seamstress* (No. 241),

respond to the world of manual labor. Leopold Gottlieb in France in *The Plasterers* (No. **83**), David Bomberg who visited Palestine in the twenties (No. 49), as well as Shalom Seba and Abraham Naton who lived there, were stimulated by new kinds of work, and often present it as an ennobling experience (Nos. **208, 174**).

The confident outlook of practical idealism

226. Johanon Simon. *Sabbath in the Kibbutz*. 1950. Oil on canvas. 25 x 19½ in. Collection Tina and Shelomo Ben-Israel, Hollis, New York.

83. Leopold Gottlieb. *Plasterers.* 1928. Oil on cardboard. 38⅝ x 27¼ in. Collection The Ein Harod Art Museum, Israel.

102. Marcel Janco. *The Wounded Soldier.* n.d. Oil on canvas, 27½ x 19¾ in. Lent by Rosenfeld Art Gallery, Tel Aviv.

and sheer optimism of Johanon Simon was not shared by Marcel Janco, who arrived in Israel in 1940 as a refugee from Romania. He was a member of the original Dada group in Zurich, which, under the impact of World War I, had rejected the forms and values of Western civilization. In Israel he attempted to integrate himself into the tasks and problems of the society of settlers and incoming refugees. There is no innocence in his paintings, no ideology, no naive belief in the resurrection of the legendary Biblical land. Instead there is the harsh reality which an experienced person encounters: the transition camps, overcrowded tent cities which cover the hills in a relentless zig-zag pattern. A painter of armed partisans, Maccabees fighting for their existence, wounded soldiers bending over their rifles—Janco does not glorify war (Nos. 97, 100, **102**, 103). Rather he sees it as part of the reality which surrounds him and which he cannot ignore.

Working in New York City in 1947, Jacques Lipchitz recognized Israel's capacity to survive and rise in *Miracle.* Simultaneously, he responded to the plight of Arabs who had fled their homes, and he created a series of sculptures on the Biblical theme of Hagar and Hagar in the Desert. The sculpture *Miracle II* (No. **144**, p. 64) is drawn from the theme of *Exodus* and poetically evokes the menorah's origin in the cosmic tree, and its transformation by Judaism. The miracle is equated with the ability of the ancient tree to continue to bloom. The menorah has returned to its original source—a spreading tree—whose trunk has been opened to reveal the Tablets of the Law. A man kneels before it, simultaneously imploring, supporting, and protecting it. Lipchitz expressed this triple role by merging the man's legs with the roots of the tree. Man, Torah and Tree, all derive sustenance from one another. The miracle does not occur by itself; it is man who produced it by his own effort. The sculpture offers a striking analogy to the ancient representation of the man in armor carrying the Menorah on his head in the catacomb of Beth Shearim in Israel. Lipchitz studied examples of ancient Jewish art that had been unearthed.

The associations evoked by *Miracle II* stem from its form and its organic unity. The arms of the Menorah rise in a V-like form on both sides of the Tablets of the Law. The branches are deeply cut, and a similar shape is shared by the buds and the man's arms and hands. The V-shape is repeated in horizontal form in the Tablets of the Law, which recede and meet at an angle. It is inverted in the man's feet and in the larger folds of his garment as they fall from his shoulders to his sides. The texture of the whole is rough, leaving the strong imprint of the artist's modeling.

The work of Naftali Bezem and Abraham Ofek, who came to Israel as youths, is saturated

179. Abraham Ofek. *Villagers.* 1969. Oil on canvas. 64 x 52 in. Lent by the artist, Jerusalem.

with the experience of emigration and settlement. The lives of both were affected by the apocalyptic events of mass migration following the Second World War. These events transformed Israel from an intimate, pioneering society, bent upon the creation of a national culture, into a melting pot of Jews from North Africa and Asia; a haven for refugees and survivors of concentration camps in Europe; and finally into a beleaguered nation. Bezem is haunted by the trauma of the emigrants arriving in small boats with their meager belongings. In his paintings, newly arrived refugees step from the boat, and kiss the earth or embrace a stinging cactus plant (Nos. 44, 45).

While many of the younger generation Israeli artists choose to enter the mainstream of modern art, and thus, like others in international art centers, have largely been preoccupied with formal problems, Bezem and Ofek rooted their art in the landscape and life of the people which they intimately experienced.

Ofek creates compositions with figures commonly referred to in Israel as "the other Israel", or "the second Israel". In his paintings, people are like plants which have been uprooted from their native habitat but have not yet struck

new roots (Nos. 177, 178, **179**). They do not seem to belong to their new country. They are unwilling settlers who do not love the earth. They are disoriented, inarticulate and grotesque. Their gestures, like their bodies, are heavy, slow, and disproportioned. They are a people who have struggled all their lives to exist. Now their struggle is with authority, with the soil, with their neighbors, with their family and with themselves. These conflicts distort their posture and their gait. Their strength seems to lie in their patient submission to fate, in being rooted in themselves, in their limited awareness of the world. They are a silent people. They speak the language of instinct and substitute gaze, touch, and inarticulate gesture for words. Their needs are basic, they seem at their best when they turn to ancient rituals, still potent and imbued with the serious primitive religious acts which guide them through a confused insecure world.

In contrast to an earlier generation, Ofek paints life as he experienced it when he arrived in Israel on a fully-packed boat from his native Bulgaria during a time of extreme hardship following the War of 1948. He represents Israel as a crude network of brutal necessities, and bares life at its nodal points: birth, marriage, death, departure, wandering and arrival. There is a strong awareness of the solitariness of man and the ambivalence of human relations—a strong sense of closeness and distance. He paints man in relation to other men, in relation to his neighbor, his cat, his cow, his hut, his yard, his table, his chair, and his bread. There are influences of Picasso, Diego Rivera and Jankel Adler, as well as traces of Jean Dubuffet and Candido Portinari. There is also simple humor in the treatment of his figures and the love with which he depicts the domesticated animals, which suggests the influence of Bulgarian folk tales and the stories of the Yiddish writers like Sholom Aleichem and Mendele Mocher Sefarim. Like the disfigurement and stunting we often encounter in their characters, Ofek's grotesque figures manifest severe incongruities.

There is a Jerusalem which is an idea and not a specific location, which embodies ascent and the quest for redemption. A Jerusalem which is in the heart, in dreams, in the sky—not of this earth. A Jerusalem which vanishes and is built, vanishes again, and is built again, until it resembles heaven.

Leopold Krakauer and Anna Ticho express in their landscapes the yearning for the ideal Jerusalem. Their Jerusalem is outside the city, in the barren, gently curved hills that evoke the unspoiled dreams of their youth. In Krakauer's drawing, thistles which grow in the parched fields in late summer are transformed and elevated into suns. They are symbols of pain and sources of solace and warmth. They are dry and twisted, tenacious and unyielding like the thorny path to the sun (Nos. 122, 123, **124,** 245, 246, 247).

Mordecai Ardon, once a pupil at the Bauhaus in Weimar, carried Jerusalem in his heart and could not rid himself of it. He personifies that peculiar blend of rationalism and mysticism which Jewish tradition so often produces. Like his father, a Hasid, Ardon searches for the hidden sparks that dwell in the most humble objects, and seeks to unite them with the heavenly light. He admired Rembrandt and El Greco, and felt a strong affinity to Klee, the mystic, and to Feininger, the metaphysician. Ardon spiritualizes physical matter. The sources he draws from are varied; the rich vocabulary of modern art transmitted through Otto Dorfner and his teachers at the Bauhaus, the dramatic

124. Leopold Krakauer. *Sun and Thistles.* 1952. Chalk on paper, 22 x 30¼ in. Collection Trude Dothan, Jerusalem.

sense of Max Reinhardt and the spiritual ferment of Weimar, Berlin and Paris during the twenties. All this is filtered through and fused with the rich store of childhood memories and Jewish learning he gathered at his home in Turov, Galicia. In his father's workshop the hand of the different clocks used to show different hours, and as a child Ardon marvelled that at some time they all struck at the same time. The mature Ardon brings the past, the present, and the future together. From 1933, when he intended to go to Paris, but landed shipwrecked in Jerusalem, he has drawn from the literature and art of Sumer and Babylonia, the Bible, the Kabala, Hebrew illuminated manuscripts, and from the dry rocks of the desert.

Ardon's problem has been defined as that of a European painter who decided to remain a Jew. Always admiring and attracted to apollonian and dionysian Athens, he found Jerusalem "ascetic with sackcloth on its head." Jerusalem, the overbearing, with its moral injunctions and demands about widows, orphans and the oppressed, did not let him accept the concept of the absolute autonomy of art. "Like a black woodpecker, Jerusalem knocks at your bark: thou . . . thou . . . thou . . . as if life could be lived only in the thou . . . That's the problem: the 'you' does not play any part in modern art. Artists are suns revolving on their own axes." [35]

Ardon looks at the universe through a transparency tinged by the Jewish mystic tradition. He uses the vocabulary of abstract art, but he is not satisfied with formal problems alone. His work touches that of Barnett Newman, Mark Rothko, and Adolph Gottlieb. They too do not restrict themselves to formal problems, since subject matter is crucial to them. Is it possible that because they are related to the Hebraic tradition, they look for a moral frame of reference and that the "Thou" is essential to them?

Ardon's shapes and signs suggest something that exists potentially. In *Negev, Train of Numbers,* (No. 16), *In the Beginning* (No. 14), *The Tents of Judea* (No. 15), he makes visible what one does not see. He is on the track of the timeless, the numinous, and is conscious that he works under the Biblical sky in the Biblical land. But as we have said, being a European artist who has decided to remain a Jew, Ardon found it difficult to paint the daily life of Palestine. He also could not paint symbols because they divest the unknown of its secret. His paintings are the pilgrimage of a modern mystic, who attempts to lift the veil, to reach the Gates of Light, although he is not sure if there is anything to be found beyond them. Search and creation are the substance of his pilgrimage; therefore, the process of his work is long, a slow unfolding of ideas, associations, a slow lifting of the veil. They are not religious pictures in the traditional sense, they breathe a pantheistic humanist spirit, but

they remain centered in the Biblical landscape. They are the work of a modern Jew who went through assimilation, enlightenment, and nationalism, but decided to remain a Jew and take from tradition that with which he could live.

Homage to Jerusalem, one of several large triptychs Ardon has created, places Jerusalem at the center of religious experience. Jerusalem is the place where ladders were erected which stood on the ground but reached to heaven, a place where ladders fell, parchments and scrolls of ancient teaching were written, of lamenting nails which allude to the Crucifixion. The painting is a poem about Jerusalem. Ladders are related to the ladder of Jacob, to heavenly ascent. The paintings can be seen as parables of the fate of man, his effort to rise and his unavoidable fall, his illusions and disillusions. The ladder also has an intense personal meaning for Ardon. When he returned to Turov after having finished his studies, an uncle came to congratulate him: "What did you study?" he asked. When Ardon answered that he had become a painter, the uncle looked around the room and inquired: "So, where is your ladder?"

The Cabalistic Sphere by Luise Kaish (No. **107**) evolves from a personal mystical attitude nourished by the cosmic imagery of the Zohar, and the Psalms, and from her form–giving energy which constantly interprets, elaborates, and shapes her spiritual experience. In the Kabalistic literature, the spheres are manifestations of the hidden process of divine life, which flow directly from the *Ein Sof* (infinite), and mediate between God and the Universe.

Yehoshua Kovarsky, in *Temple Above the Moon* (No. **120**, p. 31) and *A Time to Die and a Time to Live* (No. 121), approaches the poetry of the mythological, archaic domain of the Biblical world, and establishes contact with its spirits.

Moshe Castel's *Simchat Torah in the Ari Synagogue* (No. 56) and *Sephardic Wedding Feast* (No. 55), with their pronounced vaulted architecture, evoke the mystic experience of communal prayer. His mixed–media paintings echo ancient Babylonian clay tablets and stone inscriptions. The textures evoke processes which relate to archaeological efforts at unearthing the past. Castel locates his roots in the ancient Near East (Nos. 54, **57**, p. 51).

Barnett Newman, Adolph Gottlieb and Mark Rothko, painters of the New York School, react in their mature work, created after World War II, to the crisis of faith. Like other American painters, they felt that the ideas and ideologies which shaped the form and content of American art of the previous decade were obsolete. The War and its aftermath had shattered the very foundations upon which their art was built. By exposing the limits of human rationality, the War had shown the irrational to be a constant and powerful presence in human nature. The artists

176. Barnett Newman. *Joshua.* 1950. Oil on canvas. 36 x 25 in. Collection Mrs. Samuel Weiner, New York.

Separation of Day from Night from Haggadah of Sarajevo. Spanish manuscript, mid-14th century. National Museum, Sarajevo, Jugoslavia.

30. Leonard Baskin. *The Four Mystics.* 1952. Woodcut. 19½ x 12 in. Lent by Galerie Sumers, New York.

Mark Rothko. *Green and Maroon*. 1953. Oil on canvas. 90¾ x 54½ in. Collection The Phillips Collection, Washington, D.C.

now rejected the ideas and attitudes of Social Realism, Regionalism, Geometric Abstraction and all styles derived from faith in technology and the values of mass culture. To construct a meaningful universe, the artists turned to themselves and their private visions. The presence in New York during World War II of major European artists and leaders of the Surrealist movement opened new avenues of exploration to American artists. Automatism and biomorphism, because of their organic and therefore human–like formal aspects, became a basis from which they could move. For these artists, subject matter was of utmost importance,

and they considered abstract art practiced for its own sake a futile exercise, built on a slogan of purism. "There is no such thing as good painting about nothing," declared Gottlieb and Rothko in a letter Newman helped to draft to *The New York Times*. "We assert that the subject is crucial and only that subject matter is valid which is tragic and timeless." [36]

For these painters, art was an adventure into an unknown world. They attempted to transcend the here and now, to approach the absolute. Their paintings are religious in that they aim to touch elemental cosmic forces, and to penetrate the universe to reach a metaphysical understanding.

Newman's paintings consist of a single flat color divided by one or more bands of contrasting or complementary colors which transform the canvas into two or more rectangles that have a definite scale, expanse, and proportion, but are devoid of imagery. They have been called color field paintings. The canvas—its shape, its height and length, its color field, offers a sacred environment which engulfs the viewer and summons him to an act of contemplation.

By their stern quality, their lack of atmosphere or tactile details, by the strict intellectual approach, by their quest for the absolute and its inherent antagonism to the image, these paintings attack the sensuous nature of Western art at its very roots, and seek to divorce the act of painting from its European tradition. A theoretician of considerable originality, Newman wrote during the War years, "the new painter desires to transcend the plastic elements in art. He is declaring that the art of Western Europe is a voluptuous art first, an intellectual art by accident. He is reversing the situation by declaring that art is an expression of the mind first, and whatever sensuous elements are involved are incidental to that expression. The new painter is therefore the true revolutionary, the real leader, who is placing the artist's function on its rightful plane of the philosopher and the pure scientist, who is exploring the world of ideas, not the world of senses. Just as we get a vision of the cosmos through the symbols of a mathematical equation, just as we get a vision of truth in terms of abstract metaphysical concepts, so the artist is today giving us a vision of the world of truth in terms of visual symbols." [37]

In his stubborn search for a grand theme for modern art, which should express the sublime, pure ideas, and abstract philosophical concepts, he was impelled toward an abstract art. In his search, Newman focused on the process of the creative action of nature, and equated the creation of a new art with the process of creation itself. He fell back on Biblical and Kabalistic ideas with which he was familiar, and which offered him a ready source for his intellectual and metaphysical speculations. Newman worked in the classic "No graven image" tradition of Judaism not because images are forbidden, but because the absolute cannot be rendered by an image. It is a purely abstract conception, imageless, like the Jewish God.

If there were a Jewish art, Newman's work would be regarded as its most authentic and classic expression.

It is not accidental that the stark simplifications of his canvas has a precedent in the fourteenth century Spanish Haggadah of Sarajevo, where the separation of day from night in *Genesis* is realized by a similar abstract color field (see illustration). Thomas B. Hess, points to the deep attachment which Newman felt for the Kabala, and the crucial part it played in the formation of his art and subject matter. [38] Thus, the *Onement* series suggests completion, harmony, and also "At Onement"—the day of remembering the dead, which was for the Kabalists the ideal moment for meditation on the secrets of the Messianic act of redemption and resurrection. The *Onement* paintings intimate also the separation of day from night, the creation of Adam and the creative union of Adam and Eve.

Titles of Newman's work suggest the measure of his involvement with Biblical and Kabalistic lore: *Day One, Day Before One, Tzimtzum, Primordial Light, Uriel, White Fire, Black Fire, Cathedra, Gate, Word, Here, Voice, Abraham, Joshua* (No. **176**). The titles are metaphors of ideas and feelings which preoccupied Newman during the process of their creation.

Unlike Ardon's mysticism, which is centered on Jerusalem, Barnett Newman, who was born in New York City, and was at home in the community of New York artists, echoes in his paintings the Jewish mysticism of the Zohar, and of the Ari Hakadosh, Rabbi Isaac Luria of Safed. His work relates to the cosmology of *Or Ein Sof,* (the unending light), to open and hidden symmetries, contraction and expansion and the breaking and repairing of vessels. Hess writes: "Being Jewish was a part of his past and of his present; he was heir to a culture, and took delight in studying it—more delight than he did in studying other religions. One could say that all civilizations and sciences were like an enormous museum through which he loved to wander, and among his favorite galleries were those devoted to Jewish myths and customs, philosophers and artists, and especially to that remarkable fusion of mysticism and logic that is known as the Kabbala, and to the men who for over two thousand years contributed to its insights." [39]

The inclusion of Adolph Gottlieb in this exhibition poses a problem. There is in his work a religious quest, a journey into the unknown regions of myth, dreams and planets. His works have universal and pantheistic overtones and one might fail to find any points of reference to Jewish experience (Nos. 79, 80, 81, 82). The same might be said about the work of Gabo, Pevsner, Lipton or Lissitsky (Nos. 78, 187, 147, 151). [40] But certainly the full participation in the intellectual, scientific, artistic work of this century is in itself a major aspect of Jewish experience.

The presence of Mark Rothko's work in the exhibition is less problematic: we are confronted with a highly personal statement that brings us close to the world of ritual and icons (see illustration). Rothko's diffuse, rectangular configurations float in a hazy color field and echo the edges of the canvas. Their soft blurred contours melt into ambiguous space, rather than setting themselves off against a distinct background. The thinly painted shapes vibrate and breathe, advance and recede as if moved by

185. Leonid Pasternak. *Max Lieberman Opening Exhibition of the Academy in Berlin.* 1930. Oil on canvas. 38⅝ x 30⅜ in. Collection The Tel Aviv Museum of Art.

an unseen hand, and leave an after-image. By eliminating line, movement, and imagery from these paintings and by reducing them to shape, color and space, the artist has dematerialized them. The paintings induce an atmosphere of silence, solemnity, meditation, and transcendence; they mirror the thoughts and feelings which the spectator brings to them. In their bright yellow, deep red, dark blue, or grey variations, these paintings evoke the mysterious and the luminous; they create somber, repetitive spaces of otherness—abstract icons of sacred pathos.

Rothko's art has been interpreted in terms of withdrawal from the affairs of the world, from involvement in social and political issues, an escape from the noise of the media. It has also been seen as being influenced by the wide-open landscapes, clouds and mist-filled spaces the artist experienced in his native Oregon.

His paintings have evoked for many the Orphic cycles of death and resurrection, entrances to tombs and open sarcophagi. However, most critics agree that Rothko's paintings convey a world in which the numinous and the spiritual experience dominate. While these are generalized in Rothko's work, it is interesting to note that the German art historian Werner Haftmann points to Rothko's Jewish background as a major factor in the emergence of the artist's style. He compares the advancing and receding planes of his canvases to doors and corridors, which at one moment invite one to look and then, immediately, draw the veil. He likens them to "silently animated, stirring, concealing drapery," which are ancient Jewish metaphors for the hidden God of whom it was forbidden to make an image; to veils in the Biblical tent of meeting and the Temple curtain before the Holy of Holies (which existed only as emptiness), and to the woven canvas of the Mosaic tent. "The painter in his imagination renewing itself daily, undertook the erection of that tent which the

Jews, a nomadic people, raised around their ark in order to establish a space for the Holy in which there existed only the void and the word. From these images derive his pictures." [41] Haftmann continues, "Clearly we do not confront real 'pictures' in our classic humanistic terms. They are meditation veils, icons, tablets of contemplation, decorated tent canvases, which shelter the Numinous. With his 'image', Rothko created a new type of votive picture which in its mythic religious space is the counterpart of the esthetic icon of Mondrian. In the face of these works, an amazing fact should become clear to historians, namely that Judaism, which for 2000 years remained 'imageless', has found in our century—with the help of the meditative process of modern art—a pictorial expression of its own, a Jewish art of its own. And this at the same time when Israel was re-established as their ancient home." [42]

Haftmann's statement may have to be qualified by additional considerations. He may be overstating his point by reducing Rothko's work to Jewish sources. Yet it is interesting that this interpretation comes from a German scholar,

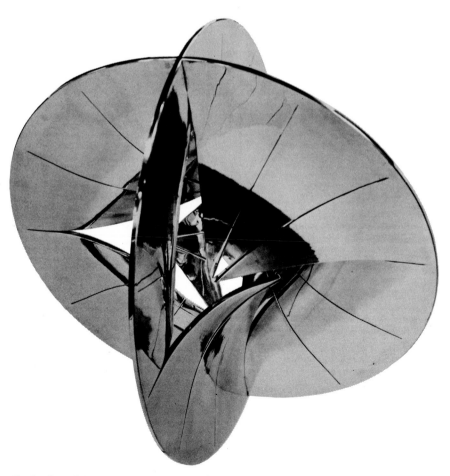

107. Luise Kaish. *The Cabalistic Sphere.* 1975. Polished aluminum, 39 x 39 in. Lent by the artist, New York.

who might be particularly sensitive to Jewish aspects of modern art. Rothko himself never gave us any clues concerning his work.

The failure to recognize specific Jewish elements in 20th art stems largely from a prejudice of modern historiography which studies history in terms of nation states and often ignores the strength of those cultures in Europe whose history is not bounded by political geography. The culture of the Jews of Eastern Europe transcends political borders so that Jews of Poland, Lithuania, Romania, the Ukraine, and other nation states shared a pervasive identity and language and had more in common with one another than they did with the ethnic majorities of the countries in which they lived. From the late 19th century the culture of the Jews of Eastern Europe spread across Western Europe, South Africa, North and South America, and Australia and they sustained their ties through their common psychic structures, their language,

their religious traditions, their publishing houses, and their unique historical consciousness.

Is it also possible that, in addition to the presence of real cultural barriers, there exists an attitude of ambivalence on the part of many artists, art historians, critics, collectors and dealers that has discouraged a thorough examination of Jewish sources in modern art? This syndrome, which suggests social and psychological processes of repression, combined with a profit-motivated attitude which carefully manages and controls public impressions, has possibly kept these sources from surfacing. Such thoughts are not new to the twentieth century.[43]

This exhibition will undoubtedly shed light on some hitherto unexamined relationships in 20th century art. By assembling these works in a communal context, and thereby revealing the sources from which they emerge, we hope that the viewer might recognize some aspects of himself.

Notes

1. Although there have been several attempts to define "Jewish Art" in terms of its unique qualities, I believe the phrase has been traditionally used more as a convenience than for purposes of clarification, and no amount of discussion about whether or not such an art exists will discourage the historian's use of this questionable yet convenient term. Therefore, Martin Buber's observations, made at the beginning of the century, are still largely applicable even after the establishment of the Jewish State.
"Und will man unter jüdischer Kunst nicht wie ich etwas Werdendes, im Entstehen Begriffenes, Unfertiges verstehen, sondern etwas Bestehendes, in sich Geschlossenes, Vollendetes, dann müsste ich auf die Frage nach dem Vorhandensein einer nationalen Kunst bei uns mit einem Nein antworten. Was uns dazu fehlt, ist der einheitliche Zusammenhang der Künstler, sowohl untereinander, als mit dem Volke selbst und dessen Idealen. Eine nationale Kunst braucht einen Erdboden, aus dem sie hervorwächst, und einen Himmel, dem sie entgegenblüht. Wir Juden von heute haben keines von beiden. Wir sind die Sklaven vieler Erden und zu verschiedenen Himmeln fliegen unsere Gedanken auf. Im tiefsten Seelengrunde aber haben wir keine Erde und keinen Himmel. Wir haben kein Volksland, das unsere Hoffnungen im Schosse trüge und dem Schreiten unserer Füsse Festigkeit verliehe, und wir haben keine Volksonne, die unsere Saaten segnete und unseren Tag vergoldete. Eine nationale Kunst braucht eine einheitliche Menschengemeinschaft, aus der sie stammt und für die sie da ist. Wir aber haben nur Stücke einer Gemeinsamkeit, und leise erst regt es sich in den Teilen, zu einem Leibe zu werden.

Nur mit der fortschreitenden Wiedergeburt kann die jüdische Kunst werden und wachsen. Eine vollendete jüdische Kunst wird erst auf jüdischem Boden möglich sein, ebenso wie eine vollendete jüdische Kultur überhaupt."
[It is not possible for a fully realized Jewish art to develop in a physical or psychological Diaspora. Such a national art requires a common origin and experience for its artists, and as such can exist only on Jewish soil and within a wholly Jewish culture.]
Martin Buber, in a speech of 1901, as quoted in H. Strauss, *Die Kunst der Juden im Wandel der Zeit und Umwelt*, Tübingen, 1972, 118-119.

2. U.Z. Greenberg, ["Drachim Bemaárav"], *Rimon* [*Hebrew Journal for Arts and Letters*], No. 6, 1924, [19-21].

3. L.V. Snowman, *Tchernichovski and His Poetry*, London, 1929, 41.

4. "It was from this Jewish tradition that the first post-Revolutionary experiments in typography, which are among the first examples of 'modern' typographical design, were done."
C. Gray, *The Great Experiment: Russian Art 1863–1922*, London, 1962, 248.

5. Lissitzky must have felt that an abstract style, a synthesis between Suprematism and Constructivism, was most compatible with the ideas of the Revolution. His interest waned in creating a national Jewish style based on Jewish folk art. In 1923 he wrote enthusiastically about the Synagogue in Mohilev and its paintings, which he and Ryback had studied; but he also stated that a national art cannot be created at will but must develop unconsciously and spontaneously from natural conditions—from a real life situation. He is

critical of the position he held previously and explains his abandonment of that position. Lissitsky was in Berlin from 1921 to 1928 and was active with David Sterenberg in the organization of the Russian exhibition of 1922.
El L. [El Lissitsky], ["The Synagogue in Mohilev"], *Rimon [Hebrew Journal For Arts and Letters]*, No. 3, 1923, [9-12].

6. O. Lubomirski as quoted in F. Meyer, *Marc Chagall*, New York, [1963], 294.

7. M. Wheeler, *Soutine*, New York, 1950, 37.

8. W. George, "The School of Paris", in C. Roth, *Jewish Art*, Greenwich, Connecticut, 1971, 229-260.

9. E. Fauré, *Soutine*, Paris, 1929, 8-9.

10. M. Raynal, *Modern French Painters*, translated by Ralph Roeder, New York, 1928, 152.

11. Raynal, *Modern French Painters*, 151.

12. W. George, *Soutine*, Paris, 1928, 15-18.

13. M. Tuchman, *Chaim Soutine*, Los Angeles, 1968, 11f.

14. R. Talpir, ["Jewish Painters of Paris"], *Gazith*, VII, No. 10, June 1945, 19-24; continued in Nos. 11-12, July-Aug. 1945, 35-44.

15. Communication with Chana Orloff.

16. Communication with Chana Orloff.

17. Meyer, *Marc Chagall*, 416.

18. Meyer, *Marc Chagall*, 416.

19. E. Roditi, "The Jewish Artist in the Modern World", in Roth, *Jewish Art*, 301.

20. A. Klapheck, *Jankel Adler*, Recklinghausen, 1966, 24.

21. Communication with Josef Herman.

22. E. Brauer, *Malerei des Fantastischen Realismus*, Munich, 1968.

23. Communication with the artist.

24. W. Schmied, *Hundertwasser*, New Zealand, 1973, 68.

25. *Harold Paris: The California Years*, P. Selz, ed., Berkeley, 1972, 28.

26. *Harold Paris*, 29.

27. Max Weber was 10 when he came from Bialystock in 1891, Louise Nevelson was 6 when she came from Kiev, Mark Rothko came from Dvinsk at the age of 10, Ben Shahn arrived from Kovno when he was 8. The three Soyers came from Borisoglepsk when Raphael and Moses Soyer were 13 years old and their brother Isaac was 6. Chaim Gross came from the Carpathian Mountains when he was 17. Many of the contemporary artists, such as Jack Levine, Abraham Rattner, Adolph Gottlieb and Barnett Newman, although born in America, were shaped by the culture of their homes which has left deep marks on their paintings.

28. Max Weber and Abraham Walkowitz, who left for Paris from the U.S. in 1905, came under the influence of Cubism, Fauvism, and primitive art, and after their return in 1909 had their first exhibitions at Gallery 291.

29. R. Soyer, *Self-Revealment; a memoir*, New York, 1969, 50-52.

30. Soyer, *Self-Revealment*, 63.

31. ". . .; but even then he would tell the story of how he realized this independence of God when he stepped over a forbidden boundary in the synagogue at Vilkomir and was not struck dead."
S. Rodman, *Portrait of the Artist as an American. Ben Shahn: A Biography with Pictures*, New York, 1951, 171-72.

32. R. Rubin, *My Life and My Art*, New York, [1970], 43.

33. Rubin, *My Life and My Art*, 53.

34. W. Herberg, "American Jewish Labor Movement" *American Jewish Yearbook*, Philadelphia, 1952.

35. Letter to W. Sandberg, In *Mordecai Ardon*, (exhibition catalogue), Jerusalem, 1963.

36. *The New York Times*, June 13, 1943, Section 2, 9.

37. T.B. Hess, *Barnett Newman*, New York, 1971, 39.

38. Hess, *Barnett Newman*, 57.

39. Hess, *Barnett Newman*, 53.

40. Gottlieb and Lipton executed numerous commissions for the design of synagogues.

41. Haftmann relates how he arrived at his insight. He came to New York City to invite Rothko to participate in *Documenta*, 1959. Rothko refused, on the grounds that he did not want to exhibit in a group show and that his work needed its own space. When Haftmann promised that this would be done, Rothko still refused and said that as a Jew he would not even think of exhibiting in Germany which had committed so many crimes against Jews. However during the conversation, Rothko remarked that he would be willing to paint, without fee, a "Chapel of Repentance" to honor the Jewish victims in hateful Germany, even if that Chapel were only a tent. This set Haftmann on the trail of his interpretation. He adds that Rothko saw in the isolated painting an example for a special conception which was to surround and absorb the whole person.
W. Haftmann, *Mark Rothko*, Düsseldorf, Städtische Kunsthalle, 1971.

42. Haftmann, *Mark Rothko*.

43. A repressive mechanism, conscious and unconscious, naive and shrewd, institutionalized and personal, is particularly effective in the visual arts. Lesser Uri, the painter, wrote at the beginning of the century:
The Jewish artist receives more encouragement from Christians than from Jews. The rich Jew shrinks from any documentation of his heritage and attempts to misdirect the thoughts of his visitor, and therefore presents him with all kinds of art works—except those by Jewish artists. Yet it is the Christian who is able to appreciate the miracle of the 3,000 year old tree which continued to produce new shoots.
[translated from the German]
L. Uri. "Thoughts About Jewish Art—Sketches and Conversations", *Ost und West*, II, 1901, 146.

57. Moshe Castel. *Tablets of the Law.* 1958. Basalt and mixed media. 63½ x 51¼ in. Lent by Mr. and Mrs. Moshe Castel, Tel Aviv.

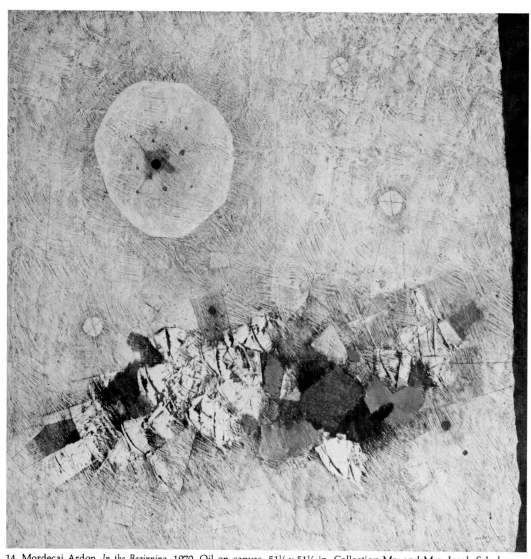

14. Mordecai Ardon. *In the Beginning.* 1970. Oil on canvas. 51¼ x 51¼ in. Collection Mr. and Mrs. Jacob Schulman, Gloversville, New York.

Catalogue of the Exhibition

Measurements: height x width x depth
* Works are illustrated in the catalogue

1. Aberdam, Alfred
Deportation, 1941-42
Oil on canvas, 47¼ x 31⅞ in. (120 x 81 cm.)
Collection The Ein Harod Art Museum, Israel

2. Adler, Jankel
Planting of Trees, 1937
Oil on canvas, 55 x 37 in. (139.5 x 94 cm.)
Collection A. J. Lax, Kent, England

3. Adler, Jankel
The Purim Players, 1931
Oil on canvas, 48⅞ x 68⅞ in. (124 x 175 cm.)
Collection The Tel Aviv Museum of Art

4. Adler, Jankel
Still Life, (Still Leben), 1928
Oil, mixed media on paper, 18¼ x 24½ in. (46 x 62 cm.)
Collection Kunstmuseum, Düsseldorf

5. Adler, Jankel
Treblinka, 1948
Oil on canvas, 60 x 36 in. (152.5 x 91.5 cm.)
Lent by Gimpel Fils Ltd., London

6. Adler, Jankel
Two Figures, 1944
Oil on canvas, 43⅞ x 33⅞ in. (111 x 86 cm.)
Collection Mr. and Mrs. Jacob Schulman, Gloversville,
New York

7. Adler, Jankel
Two Orphans, 1942
Oil on canvas, 32 x 42 in. (81 x 106.5 cm.)
Collection Josef Herman, London

8. Adler, Jankel *
Two Rabbis, 1942
Oil on canvas, 33⅞ x 44⅛ in. (85.5 x 112 cm.)
Collection The Museum of Modern Art, New York,
Gift of Sam Salz, 1949

9. Agam, Yaacov
Double Metamorphosis II, 1964
Oil on corrugated aluminum, in eleven sections, 8 ft. 10
in. x 13 ft. 3¼ in. (2.68 x 4.04 m.)
Collection The Museum of Modern Art, New York,
Gift of Mr. and Mrs. George M. Jaffin, 1965

10. Agam, Yaacov
Life is a Passing Shadow, 1970
Oil on aluminum (two sides), 28½ x 45 x 2¼ in. (72.5 x
114 x 5.7 cm.)
Collection The Museum of Art, Carnegie Institute,
Pittsburgh,
Gift of Mr. and Mrs. Harold J. Ruttenberg

11. Anonymous
Lion, (work drawing for gravestone)
Drawing, 8 x 13 in. (20.2 x 33 cm.)
Collection Boris Aronson, Grandview, New York

12. Ardon, Mordecai
Carpet of Love, 1961
Oil on canvas, 29 x 40 in. (73.5 x 101.5 cm.)
Collection Mr. and Mrs. Raphael Recanati, New York

13. Ardon, Mordecai
The Fallen, 1955-56 (triptych):
    left: *The Traps*, 60⅝ x 52 in. (154 x 132 cm.)
    center: *The House of Cards*, 59⅞ x 104 in. (152 x 264 cm.)
    right: *The Unborn*, 60⅝ x 52 in. (154 x 132 cm.)
Oil on canvas
Collection Stedelijk Museum, Amsterdam

14. Ardon, Mordecai *
In the Beginning, 1970
Oil on canvas, 51¼ x 51¼ in. (129.5 x 129.5 cm.)
Collection Mr. and Mrs. Jacob Schulman, Gloversville,
New York

15. Ardon, Mordecai
The Tents of Judea, 1950
Oil and tempera on composition board, 31⅞ x 39⅜ in.
(80.5 x 100 cm.)
Collection The Museum of Modern Art, New York,
Gift of Miss Belle Kogan, 1952

16. Ardon, Mordecai
Train of Numbers, 1963
Oil on canvas, 29 x 57⅛ in. (73.5 x 145 cm.)
Collection The Ein Harod Art Museum, Israel

17. Aronson, Boris
Sketch for Ark—(Temple Sinai)
Gouache, 22 x 17 in. (56 x 43 cm.)
Lent by the artist, Grandview, New York

18. Aronson, Boris
Untitled, 1920
Woodcut on fabric, 5¼ x 6½ in. (13.3 x 16 cm.)
Lent by the artist, Grandview, New York

19. Aronson, Boris *
Untitled, n.d.
Woodcut on paper, 14 x 11 in. (35.5 x 28 cm.)
Lent by the artist, Grandview, New York

20. Aronson, David
Dispute II, n.d.
Encaustic, 42 x 48 in. (106.5 x 122 cm.)
Lent by the artist, Sudbury, Massachusetts

21. Aronson, David
The Golem, 1958
Encaustic, 57 x 64 in. (145 x 162.5 cm.)
Lent by the artist, Sudbury, Massachusetts

22. Aronson, David
Teacher and Student I, 1972
Encaustic, 48 x 30 in. (122 x 76 cm.)
Lent by the artist, Sudbury, Massachusetts

23. Bak, Samuel
The Family, 1974
Oil on canvas, 65 x 90 in. (160 x 200 cm.)
Collection Susan T. and Joachim J. Aberbach, New
York

24. Bak, Samuel
Group with Captive Angel, 1973
Oil on canvas, 52½ x 39¼ in. (130 x 97 cm.)
Collection Dr. Frank M. Purnell, New York

25. Bak, Samuel
Point of Departure (Izcor), 1973
Oil on canvas, 40½ x 40½ in. (103 x 103 cm.)
Private Collection, Chicago

26. Bak, Samuel
Resting Soldier, n.d.
Crayon, pastel on paper, 29½ x 21½ in. (75 x 54.5 cm.)
Collection Mr. and Mrs. Joseph Kahn, New York

27. Bak, Samuel *
The Traveller, 1972 (triptych):
    left: 39½ x 32 in. (100 x 81 cm.)
    center: 39½ x 39½ in. (100 x 100 cm.)
    right: 39½ x 32 in. (100 x 81 cm.)
Oil on canvas
Collection Victor Barnett, New York

28. Band, Max
Jacob and the Angel, 1943
Oil on canvas, 38 x 24¼ in. (96.5 x 61.5 cm.)
Collection The Jewish Museum, New York

29. Baskin, Leonard
Blind Rabbi, 1971
Ink drawing, 40 x 27 in. (101.5 x 68.5 cm.)
Lent by Kennedy Galleries, Inc., New York

30. Baskin, Leonard *
The Four Mystics, 1952
Woodcut, 19½ x 12 in. (49.5 x 30.5 cm.)
Lent by Galerie Sumers, New York

31. Baskin, Leonard
Job, 1972
Bronze relief, 9¼ in. diameter (23.3 cm.)
Lent by Kennedy Galleries, Inc., New York

32. Baskin, Leonard
Prayer, 1972
Bronze, 34½ in. high (87.5 cm.)
Lent by Kennedy Galleries, Inc., New York

33. Beckmann, Max *
Synagogue, 1919
Oil on canvas, 35½ x 55⅛ in. (90 x 140 cm.)
Collection Städelsches Kunstinstitut und Städtische
Galerie, Frankfurt
Acquired 1972 by gifts of citizens of Frankfurt and by
means of the city of Frankfurt

34. Ben–Zion
Friday Evening, before 1956
Oil on canvas, 42 x 25⅛ in. (106.5 x 64 cm.)
Collection The Hirshhorn Museum and Sculpture
Garden, Smithsonian Institution, Washington, D. C.

35. Ben–Zion
Jewish Bookseller, before 1956
Oil on canvas, 45¼ x 26¼ in. (114.2 x 66.7 cm.)
Collection The Hirshhorn Museum and Sculpture
Garden, Smithsonian Institution, Washington, D. C.

36. Bergner, Yosl
The Artisans, 1971
Oil on canvas, 57¼ x 88⅝ in. (145 x 225 cm.)
Lent by the artist, Tel Aviv

37. Bergner, Yosl
Betrayal, 1970
Oil on canvas, 33⅛ x 39⅜ in. (84 x 100 cm.)
Collection I. Silman, Jerusalem

38. Bergner, Yosl
Destination X, III, 1975
Oil on canvas, 19⅝ x 25⅝ in. (50 x 65 cm.)
Lent by the artist, Jerusalem

39. Bergner, Yosl *
Empty Room, 1966
Oil on canvas, 30 x 36 in. (76.2 x 91.4 cm.)
Collection Mr. and Mrs. Harold J. Ruttenberg,
Pittsburgh and Jerusalem

40. Bergner, Yosl
Flying Spice Box, 1966
Oil on canvas, 32 x 39⅜ in. (81 x 100 cm.)
Collection The Ein Harod Art Museum, Israel

41. Bergner, Yosl
Kafkaesque Figure, 1960
Oil on canvas, 51 x 31½ in. (129.5 x 80 cm.)
Collection The Jewish Museum, New York,
Gift of Herman Elkon

42. Bergner, Yosl
"There is no prophet in his town", 1969
Oil on canvas, 39⅜ x 39⅜ in. (100 x 100 cm.)
Collection Mr. and Mrs. Harold J. Ruttenberg,
Pittsburgh and Jerusalem

43. Bezem, Naftali *
Binding of Isaac (Akeda), 1968
Oil on canvas, 35⅜ x 51¼ in. (90 x 130 cm.)
Lent by the artist, Jerusalem

44. Bezem, Naftali
Gardner, 1967
Oil on canvas
Lent by the artist, Jerusalem

45. Bezem, Naftali
Man Flying with Cactus, 1970
Acrylic on canvas, 51¼ x 51¼ in. (130 x 130 cm.)
Lent by the artist, Jerusalem

46. Bloom, Hyman
The Rabbi, 1957
Gouache on paper, 19½ x 17½ in. (49.5 x 44.4 cm.)
Collection Mr. and Mrs. Jacob Schulman, Gloversville,
New York

47. Bloom, Hyman *
The Synagogue, 1940
Oil on canvas, 65¼ x 46¾ in. (165.7 x 118.1 cm.)
Collection The Museum of Modern Art, New York,
Acquired through the Lillie P. Bliss Bequest, 1943

48. Bomberg, David *
Ghetto Theatre, 1920
Oil on canvas, 30 x 25 in. (76.2 x 63.5 cm.)
Lent by Ben Uri Art Gallery, London

49. Bomberg, David
Irrigation—Zionist Development, 1923
Charcoal and chalk on paper, 22¼ x 28½ in. (56.5 x 72.3 cm.)
Lent by Fischer Fine Art Ltd., London

50. Bomberg, David
Jewish Theatre, 1913
Black chalk drawing on paper, 21¾ x 23¾ in. (54.6 x 60.3 cm.)
Collection Leeds City Art Galleries, England

51. Bornfriend, Jacob
Seder Table, 1953
Oil on canvas, 39 x 33 in. (99 x 83.8 cm.)
Collection A. J. Lax, Kent, England

52. Brauer, Erich *
Persecution of the Jewish People (7 sections), 1973-4
 Israel Besieged
 Kishinev Pogrom
 The Martyr
 1944
 Masada
 Destruction of the Temple
 Slaves were we to Pharoah in Egypt
Oil on canvas, 40 x 32 in. each (101.7 x 81.2 cm.)
Lent by the artist, Vienna

53. Budko, Joseph
Two Jewish Watercarriers, 1929
Oil on canvas, 33¼ x 35¾ in. (99.8 x 90.7 cm.)
Collection The Israel Museum, Jerusalem,
Gift of Dr. Aley Raffaeli, Jerusalem

54. Castel, Moshe
Altar, 1963
Mixed media on canvas, 5 x 4 ft. (152.5 x 122 cm.)
Collection Park Avenue Synagogue, New York

55. Castel, Moshe
Sephardic Wedding Feast, n.d.
Oil on canvas, 21¼ x 28¾ in. (54 x 73 cm.)
Collection The Tel Aviv Museum of Art

56. Castel, Moshe
Simchat Torah in the Ari Synagogue, n.d.
Oil on canvas, 29 x 21½ in. (73.6 x 54.6 cm.)
Lent by Rosenfeld Art Gallery, Tel Aviv

57. Castel, Moshe *
Tablets of the Law, 1958
Basalt and mixed media, 63½ x 51¼ in. (162 x 130 cm.)
Lent by Mr. and Mrs. Moshe Castel, Tel Aviv

58. Chagall, Marc
The Dream, 1939
Gouache and pastel on composition board, 20 x 26 in. (50.8 x 66 cm.)
Collection The Phillips Collection, Washington, D.C.

59. Chagall, Marc
Feast of the Tabernacles, 1916
Gouache on paper, 13 x 16⅛ in. (33 x 41 cm.)
Private Collection

60. Chagall, Marc
Flowers in the Street—My Childhood Home, 1935
Oil on canvas, 38⅛ x 46⅝ in. (97 x 118.3 cm.)
Collection Mr. and Mrs. Yosel Rosensaft, New York

61. Chagall, Marc †
Green Violinist, 1923-4
Oil on canvas, 78 x 42¾ in. (198.1 x 108.5 cm.)
Collection The Solomon R. Guggenheim Museum, New York

62. Chagall, Marc
In the Night, 1943
Oil on canvas, 18½ x 20⅝ in. (46.9 x 52.3 cm.)
Collection Philadelphia Museum of Art,
The Louis E. Stern Collection

63. Chagall, Marc†
Lovers, 1922
Drypoint with watercolor, 10⅞ x 8½ in. (27.4 x 21.5 cm.)
Collection The Solomon R. Guggenheim Museum, New York

64. Chagall, Marc *
Over Vitebsk, 1914
Oil on paper mounted on canvas, 27½ x 35¼ in. (69.8 x 89.5 cm.)
Collection Art Gallery of Ontario, Toronto,
Gift of Sam and Ayala Zacks, 1970

65. Chagall, Marc
Praying Desk, 1909
Oil on canvas, 18¾ x 23⅞ in. (47.6 x 60.4 cm.)
Collection Yulla Lipchitz and Lolya Lipchitz, New York

66. Chagall, Marc
Purim, 1916-18
Oil on canvas, 19⅞ x 28¼ in. (50.2 x 71.7 cm.)
Collection Philadelphia Museum of Art,
The Louis E. Stern Collection

67. Chagall, Marc †
Remembrance, 1914
Mixed media on paper, 12⅝ x 8¾ in. (32 x 22.2 cm.)
Collection The Solomon R. Guggenheim Museum, New York

68. Chagall, Marc
Time is a River Without Banks (Le Temps n'a point de rive), 1930-39
Oil on canvas, 39⅜ x 32 in. (99.5 x 81.2 cm.)
Collection The Museum of Modern Art, New York,
Given anonymously, 1943

69. Chagall, Marc†
Village and Violinist, n.d.
Gouache, 13⅝ x 16⅝ in. (34.5 x 42.1 cm.)
Collection The Solomon R. Guggenheim Museum, New York

70. Chagall, Marc
Vitebsk—from Mt. Zdanov, 1917
Oil on canvas, 24½ x 32½ in. (62.2 x 82.5 cm.)
Collection Mr. and Mrs. Perry R. Pease, New York

71. Chagall, Marc
Western Wall, 1932
Oil on canvas, 28⅜ x 36¼ in. (73 x 92 cm.)
Collection The Tel Aviv Museum of Art

72. Chagall, Marc *
White Crucifixion, 1938
Oil on canvas, 61 x 55 in. (154.9 x 139.7 cm.)
Collection The Art Institute of Chicago,
Gift of Alfred S. Alschuler

73. Cherney, Marvin
Man with Torah, ca. 1957-58
Oil on canvas, 36 x 25⅞ in. (91.4 x 65.5 cm.)
Collection The Hirshhorn Museum and Sculpture Garden, Smithsonian Institution, Washington, D.C.

74. Epstein, Jacob *
East Side People, 1900-01
Chalk on paper, 26¼ x 23¼ in. (67.3 x 59 cm.)
Collection The Jewish Museum, New York,
Gift of Karl Nathan

† withdrawn by The Guggenheim Museum at the
  request of the artist.

75. Epstein, Jacob
Portrait of Einstein, 1933
Bronze, 20¾ x 11¾ x 10½ in. (52.7 x 29.8 x 26.6 cm.)
Collection The Hirshhorn Museum and Sculpture
Garden, Smithsonian Institution, Washington, D.C.

76. Etrog, Sorel
Hasidic Head, 1959-61
Bronze, 45⅝ x 43⅞ x 42⅛ in. (115.8 x 111.2 x 107.1 cm.)
Collection The Hirshhorn Museum and Sculpture
Garden, Smithsonian Institution, Washington, D.C.

77. Fima
Jerusalem, n.d.
Oil on canvas, 29 x 48 in. (73.6 x 121.9 cm.)
Collection Mrs. Olga Bineth, Jerusalem

78. Gabo, Naum
Column, 1923
Plastic, wood, metal, 41 in. high (104.2 cm.)
Collection The Solomon R. Guggenheim Museum, New
York

79. Gottlieb, Adolph
Nocturne, 1945
Oil on canvas, 26 x 31 in. (66 x 78.8 cm.)
Collection Mrs. Adolph Gottlieb, New York

80. Gottlieb, Adolph
Oedipus, c. 1942
Oil on canvas, 34 x 26 in. (86.3 x 66 cm.)
Collection Mrs. Adolph Gottlieb, New York

81. Gottlieb, Adolph
The Oracle, 1947-48
Oil on canvas, 44 x 60 in. (111.7 x 152.4 cm.)
Collection The Albert A. List Family, New York

82. Gottlieb, Adolph
Tints, 1971
Oil on canvas, 90 x 48 in. (228.6 x 121.9 cm.)
Collection Mrs. Adolph Gottlieb, New York

83. Gottlieb, Leopold *
Plasterers, 1928
Oil on cardboard, 38⅝ x 27¼ in (98 x 69 cm.)
Collection The Ein Harod Art Museum, Israel

84. Gropper, William
Refugee Woman and Baby, n.d.
Oil on paper, 14⅛ x 17 in. (36 x 43.1 cm.)
Collection The Hirshhorn Museum and Sculpture
Garden, Smithsonian Institution, Washington, D.C.

85. Gropper, William *
Tailor, 1940
Oil on canvas, 21¼ x 26¼ in. (53.9 x 66.6 cm.)
Collection The Hirshhorn Museum and Sculpture
Garden, Smithsonian Institution, Washington, D.C.

86. Gross, Chaim
East Side Girl, 1948
Lignum vitae, 48½ in. high (123.1 cm.)
Lent by Forum Gallery, New York

87. Gurvich, Jose
Chaver and Chavera, n.d.
Oil on canvas
Collection Susan T. and Joachim J. Aberbach,
New York

88. Gurvich, Jose
Purim, n.d.
Oil on canvas
Collection Susan T. and Joachim J. Aberbach,
New York

89. Harkavy, Minna
The Last Prayer, 1949
Bronze, 18 in. high (45.7 cm.)
Lent by the Whitney Museum of American Art,
New York

90. Herman, Josef
My Father, 1943
Gouache, tempera on gesso, 38 x 32 in. (96.5 x 81.2 cm.)
Lent by the artist, London

91. Herman, Josef
The Purim Players, 1943
Gouache, tempera on gesso, 30 x 40 in. (76.2 x 101.6
cm.)
Lent by the artist, London

92. Hirszenberg, Samuel *
Funeral of the Zadik, 1905
Oil on canvas, 30 x 81 in. (76.2 x 205.7 cm.)
Collection The Jewish Museum, New York

93. Hirszenberg, Samuel
Tashlich, 1907
Oil on canvas, 24 x 18½ in. (61 x 47 cm.)
Collection The Tel Aviv Museum of Art

94. Hundertwasser, Fritz
Crematoria in Procession, 1963
Mixed media on canvas, 35 x 46 in. (89 x 116 cm.)
Collection Siegfried Poppe, Hamburg

95. Hundertwasser, Fritz
House with Yellow Smoke, 1962-3
Mixed media on paper, 31⅞ x 25⅝ in. (81.3 x 64.8 cm.)
Collection Susan T. and Joachim J. Aberbach,
New York

96. Jacobson, Nathaniel
The Survivors, 1959
Acrylic and oil on canvas, 72 x 46 in. (182.8 x 116.8 cm.)
Collection Mr. and Mrs. Melvin Miller, Chesnut Hill,
Massachusetts

97. Janco, Marcel
Fighters of Ghetto Warsaw, 1948
Oil on canvas, 27 x 18½ in. (68.5 x 47 cm.)
Collection The Temple Museum of Religious and
Ceremonial Art, The Temple, Cleveland

98. Janco, Marcel
The Goat, n.d.
Oil on canvas, 25¾ x 36½ in. (65.4 x 92.7 cm.)
Lent by Rosenfeld Art Gallery, Tel Aviv

99. Janco, Marcel
Maabaroth in Grey, ca. 1950
Oil on canvas, 30¾ x 38½ in. (78.1 x 97.7 cm.)
Collection The Jewish Museum, New York,
Gift of M. R. Schwaitzer

100. Janco, Marcel
The Maccabees, 1952
Oil on canvas, 24 x 40 in. (70 x 100 cm.)
Lent by the artist, Tel Aviv

101. Janco, Marcel
The Military Parade, n.d.
Oil on canvas, 25½ x 36¼ in. (64.7 x 92 cm.)
Lent by Rosenfeld Art Gallery, Tel Aviv

102. Janco, Marcel *
The Wounded Soldier, n.d.
Oil on canvas, 27½ x 19¾ in. (69.8 x 50.1 cm.)
Lent by Rosenfeld Art Gallery, Tel Aviv

103. Janco, Marcel
Wounded Soldier in the Night, n.d.
Oil on masonite, 27¾ x 19⅞ in. (70.5 x 50.3 cm.)
Collection The Israel Museum, Jerusalem

104. Jules, Mervin
The Little Presser, 1943
Oil on composition board, 11½ x 11⅝ in.
(29.2 x 29.4 cm.)
Collection The Museum of Modern Art, New York,
Purchase, 1943

105. Kahn, Wolf
Professors Louis Finkelstein and Saul Lieberman, 1966
Acrylic on canvas, 46 x 53 in. (116.8 x 134.6 cm.)
Collection The Jewish Theological Seminary of
America, New York

106. Kaiser, Raffi
After the Battle of Mitzpeh Ramon, 1973
Tempera on canvas, 57½ x 44⅞ in. (146 x 114 cm.)
Collection Bracha and Yitzhack Rager, Mitzpeh Ramon,
Israel

107. Kaish, Luise *
The Cabalistic Sphere, 1975
Polished aluminum, 39 x 39 in. (99 x 99 cm.)
Lent by the artist, New York

108. Kaish, Luise
The Cabalistic Sphere II, 1975
Polished stainless steel, 12 x 12 x 12 in. (30.4 x 30.4 x
30.4 cm.)
Lent by the artist, New York

109. Kaish, Luise
Holocaust, 1975
Bronze, 80 x 61 x 15 in. (203.2 x 154.9 x 38.1 cm.)
Collection The Albert A. List Family, New York

110. Kantor, Morris
Farewell to Union Square, n.d.
Oil on canvas, 36 x 27 in. (91.4 x 68.6 cm.)
Collection Newark Museum of Art

111. Kaplan, Anatole
The Bewitched Tailor, 1957 (Illustration for Sholom
Aleichem story), Chapter 1, No. 8
Lithograph, 23¼ x 27⅛ in. (59.2 x 68.8 cm.)
Collection The Jewish Museum, New York

112. Kaplan, Anatole
The Bewitched Tailor, 1957 (Illustration for Sholom
Aleichem story), Chapter 4, No. 10
Lithograph, 23¼ x 27⅛ in. (59.2 x 68.8 cm.)
Collection The Jewish Museum, New York

113. Karavan, Dani
Jerusalem, 1974
Bronze, 8 x 9 ft. (2,43 x 2,74 m.)
Collection El Al Israel Airlines, New York

114. Kaufmann, Isidore
Friday Evening, ca. 1900
Oil on canvas, 28½ x 35½ in. (72.3 x 90.1 cm.)
Collection The Jewish Museum, New York

115. Kienholz, Edward
History as a Planter, 1961
Wood, metal, paper, paint, aluminum and Wandering
Jew plant, 33 x 18¾ x 12½ in. (83.8 x 47.5 x 31.7 cm.)
Collection Los Angeles County Museum of Art,
Anonymous Gift through the Contemporary Art
Council

116. Kiköine, Michael
Landscape Near Abu Gosh, n.d.
Oil on canvas, 32 x 23½ in. (81.2 x 59.6 cm.)
Collection Mrs. Olga Bineth, Jerusalem

117. Kirszenbaum, Yeheskel
Arrival of the Messiah, 1937
Oil on cardboard, 23¼ x 27¼ in. (59 x 69 cm.)
Collection The Israel Museum, Jerusalem,
Bequeathed by the Artist through Baroness Alix de
Rothschild, Paris

118. Klapish, Liliane
View of Jerusalem, 1974
Oil on canvas, 57 x 45 in. (144.7 x 112.5 cm.)
Collection Mrs. Olga Bineth, Jerusalem

119. Kovarsky, Yehoshua
Kaddish, 1961
Oil on canvas, 40 x 40 in. (101.5 x 101.5 cm.)
Collection Mrs. Corinne Kovarsky, Los Angeles

120. Kovarsky, Yehoshua *
Temple Above the Moon, 1958
Oil on canvas, 40 x 50 in. (101.5 x 127 cm.)
Collection Mr. and Mrs. Jack L. Stein, Los Angeles

121. Kovarsky, Yehoshua
A Time to Die and a Time to Live, 1955
Oil on canvas, 60 x 50 in. (152.4 x 127 cm.)
Collection Seth Glickenhaus, New York

122. Krakauer, Leopold
Hills with Thistles, n.d.
Charcoal on paper, 22 x 30⅛ in. (56 x 76.5 cm.)
Collection The Tel Aviv Museum of Art, Israel

123. Krakauer, Leopold
Judean Hills, 1947
Chalk on paper, 22 x 30¼ in.
(56 x 77 cm.)
Collection Trude Dothan, Jerusalem

124. Krakauer, Leopold *
Sun and Thistles, 1952
Chalk on paper, 22 x 30¼ in. (56 x 77 cm.)
Collection Trude Dothan, Jerusalem

125. Kramer, Jacob *
Day of Atonement, 1919
Oil on canvas, 39¼ x 48⅛ in. (99.6 x 122.4 cm.)
Collection Leeds City Art Galleries, England

126. Kuhn, Walt
Sabbath Bread, 1946
Oil on canvas, 59 x 49¼ in. (150 x 125 cm.)
Collection Mrs. Otto L. Spaeth, New York

127. Kulvianski, Issai
My Parents—I (Meine Eltern–I), 1925
Oil on canvas, 59 x 49¼ in. (150 x 125 cm.)
Collection Der Senator für Wissenschaft und Kunst,
Berlin

128. Lasansky, Mauricio
Nazi Drawings (triptych), 1965
left: 80 x 38 in. (203 x 96.5 cm.)
center: 80 x 45 in. (203 x 114.5 cm.)
right: 80 x 38 in. (203 x 96.5 cm.)
Pencil with water and turpentine base washes and
collage
Collection Richard Levitt, Des Moines

129. Lasker, Joe
Memo, 1954
Oil on masonite, 20 x 33¾ in. (50.8 x 85.7 cm.)
Lent by Kraushaar Galleries, New York

130. Lasker, Joe
Scissor Grinder, n.d.
Oil on board, 26 x 38 in. (66 x 96.5 cm.)
Collection Charles H. Renthal, New York

131. Levanon, Mordecai
Landscape, 1966
Gouache on paper mounted on cardboard,
39½ x 27½ in. (100 x 70 cm.)
Collection The Israel Museum, Jerusalem

132. Levine, David
The Pressers, 1968
Oil on board, 10¼ x 9½ in. (26 x 23.4 cm.)
Lent by Forum Gallery, New York

133. Levine, David
Women Pressing, 1966
Watercolor on paper, 10½ x 14½ in. (26.6 x 36.8 cm.)
Collection Mrs. Janet Cantor, New York

134. Levine, Jack
Jewish Cantors in the Synagogue, 1930
Crayon and chalk, 17 x 11½ in. (47.5 x 32.5 cm.)
Collection The Fogg Art Museum, Harvard University,
Cambridge, Massachusetts,
Bequest of Dr. Denman W. Ross

135. Levine, Jack *
The Passing Scene, 1941
Oil on board, 48 x 29¾ in. (121.9 x 75.5 cm.)
Collection The Museum of Modern Art, New York,
Purchase, 1942

136. Levine, Jack
Planning Solomon's Temple, 1940
Oil on masonite, 10 x 8 in. (25.2 x 20.2 cm.)
Collection The Israel Museum, Jerusalem,
Gift of Mrs. Rebecca Schulman

137. Levine, Jack
Tombstone Cutter, 1947
Oil on canvas, 30 x 36 in. (76.2 x 90 cm.)
Collection Mr. and Mrs. Jacob Schulman, Gloversville,
New York

138. Levine, Jack
Warsaw Ghetto, 1969
Lithograph, 23¼ x 30 in. (59 x 76.2 cm.)
Lent by Kennedy Galleries, Inc., New York

139. Levine, Jack
White Horse, 1946
Oil on canvas, 30 x 36 in. (76.2 x 90 cm.)
Collection Museum of Art, The University of
Oklahoma, Norman

140. Levitan, Isaac Ilyich
On the Way to Zion, n.d.
Oil on paper, 11⅞ x 7½ in. (30 x 18.5 cm.)
Collection The Israel Museum, Jerusalem,
Gift of Professor Schorr

141. Liebermann, Max
Portrait of Professor Hermann Cohen, 1913
Oil on canvas, 35 x 28¾ in. (89 x 73 cm.)
Collection The Israel Museum, Jerusalem

142. Lilien, Ephraim Moses
Abraham and Isaac, n.d.
Ink on paper, 16 x 13½ in. (40.6 x 34.2 cm.)
Collection Mrs. Olga Bineth, Jerusalem

143. Linke, Bronislaw
Circus, 1955-58
Oil on canvas, 59 x 47 in. (149.5 x 119.5 cm.)
Collection National Museum, Warsaw

144. Lipchitz, Jacques *
Miracle II, 1947
Bronze, 30½ x 14 in. (77.4 x 35.5 cm.)
Collection The Jewish Museum, New York,
Gift of Karl Nathan

145. Lipchitz, Jacques
Sacrifice, 1949-57
Bronze, 44½ in. high (113 cm.)
Collection The Jewish Museum, New York,
Gift of The Albert A. List Family

146. Lipton, Seymour
Manuscript, 1961
Brazed bronze on monel metal, 63⅜ x 84⅛ x 37⅛ in.
(161 x 213.8 x 94.4 cm.)
Collection The Museum of Modern Art, New York

147. Lipton, Seymour
The Pioneer, 1957
Nickel silver on monel metal, 94 x 32 in. (238.7 x 81.2 cm.)
Lent by The Metropolitan Museum of Art, New York
Gift of Mrs. Albert A. List, 1958, subject to life interest

148. Lissitsky, El *
Study for cover from Chad Gadya, 1917
Brush, gouache, pen and ink, traces of pencil, 11 x 9 in.
(28 x 22.9 cm.)
Collection The Museum of Modern Art, New York

149. Lissitsky, El
*Study for "Came the fire and burnt the stick" from Chad
Gadya,* 1917
Brush, pen and ink, traces of pencil, 11⅛ x 9 in. (28.1 x
22.9 cm.)
Collection The Museum of Modern Art, New York

150. Lissitsky, El
*Study for "Came the slaughterer and slaughtered the
ox" from Chad Gadya,* 1917
Brush, gouache, pen and ink, traces of pencil, 11 x 9 in.
(27.3 x 22.9 cm.)
Collection The Museum of Modern Art, New York

151. Lissitsky, El
Proun Composition, ca. 1922
Gouache and ink, 19¾ x 15¾ in. (50.2 x 40 cm.)
Collection The Museum of Modern Art, New York,
Gift of Curt Valentin

152. Lissitsky, El *
Lion (from Synagogue of Mohilev wall painting),
ca. 1916
Watercolor and charcoal, 9 x 9½ in. (22.8 x 24.1 cm.)
Collection Boris Aronson, Grandview, New York

153. Lissitsky, El
*Zodiac–Archer (from Synagogue of Mohilev wall
painting),* ca. 1916
Watercolor and charcoal, 11 x 11 in. (27.9 x 27.9 cm.)
Collection Boris Aronson, Grandview, New York

154. Lozowick, Louis
Chicago, 1923
Oil on canvas, 22 x 70½ in. (55.8 x 179 cm.)
Collection Lee Lozowick, Parsippany, New Jersey

155. Lozowick, Louis
The Concrete Mixer, 1939
Oil on canvas, 24 x 18 in. (60.9 x 45.7 cm.)
Collection Mrs. Adele Lozowick, Milburn, New Jersey

156. Lozowick, Louis
Lone Worshipper, 1966
Casein, 14 in. diameter (35.5 cm.)
Collection Dr. and Mrs. Henry Fogelman, Stamford,
Connecticut

157. Lozowick, Louis
New York, 1926-27
Oil on canvas, 29¾ x 21¾ in. (75.5 x 55.2 cm.)
Collection Walker Art Center, Minneapolis, Minnesota
Gift of Hudson D. Walker, Minneapolis

158. Lozowick, Louis
Urban Geometry, 1925-27
Oil on canvas, 30 x 22 in. (76.2 x 55.8 cm.)
Collection Lee Lozowick, Parsippany, New Jersey

159. Mané-Katz
The Mill, 1960
Oil on canvas, 54 x 45 in. (137.1 x 114.3 cm.)
Collection Mr. and Mrs. Raphael Recanati, New York

160. Manievich, Abraham
Rumour of Pogrom, 1917
Oil on cardboard and wood, 14½ x 17¾ in. (37 x 45 cm.)
Collection Ein Harod Museum of Art, Israel

161. Maryan, Maryan S.
Figure with Upraised Arms, 1963
Oil on canvas, 29 x 24 in. (73.6 x 60.9 cm.)
Collection The Jewish Museum, New York,
Gift of Mrs. Rose Cohoron

162. Maryan, Maryan S.
Personage on Blue Ground, 1969
Oil on canvas, 50 x 50 in. (127 x 127 cm.)
Lent by Allan Frumkin Gallery, New York

163. Maryan, Maryan S. *
Personage, Man with Donkey Ears, 1962
Oil on canvas, 50 x 50 in. (127 x 127 cm.)
Lent by Allan Frumkin Gallery, New York

164. Menkes, Sigmund
Cohanim Blessing, 1964
Oil on canvas, 51 x 40 in. (129 x 101.6 cm.)
Collection Mr. and Mrs. Jacob Schulman, Gloversville,
New York

165. Menkes, Sigmund
The Trial, 1940
Oil on canvas, 52 x 76 in. (132 x 193 cm.)
Lent by the artist, Riverdale, New York

166. Menkes, Sigmund *
The Uplifting of the Torah, 1928
Oil on canvas, 86 x 65 in. (218.4 x 165.1 cm.)
Private collection

167. Menkes, Sigmund *
Uprising of Ghetto Warsaw, 1943
Oil on canvas, 41 x 25 in. (104.1 x 63.5 cm.)
Lent by the artist, Riverdale, New York

168. Minkowsky, Mauricy
"He cast a look and was hurt" (Hatzitz Ve'Hanifgah), 1910
Oil on canvas, 29 x 42 in. (73.6 x 106.6 cm.)
Collection The Jewish Museum, New York,
Gift of Mrs. Rose Mintz

169. Mintchine, Abraham
Landscape near Cagnes (Environs de Cagnes), 1931
Oil on canvas, 39¼ x 32 in. (99.6 x 81.2 cm.)
Lent by Gimpel Fils Ltd., London

170. Mintchine, Abraham *
Self Portrait, 1926
Oil on canvas, 31⅞ x 21 in. (81 x 53.5 cm.)
Collection The Israel Museum, Jerusalem

171. Modigliani, Amedeo
Seated Nude (Caryatid), 1914
Watercolor wash, pencil, 21¼ x 16⅜ in. (53.9 x 41.1 cm.)
Collection The Museum of Modern Art, New York,
Gift of Mrs. Saidie A. May

172. Moreh, Mordecai
Circus Duel (Duel dans un cirque), 1966
Etching, 14¾ x 20¾ in. (37.5 x 52.5 cm.)
Collection The Tel Aviv Museum of Art, Israel

173. Myers, Jerome *
Street Market, 1917
Oil on fiberboard, 24⅞ x 29¾ in. (62.9 x 75.5 cm.)
Collection The Hirshhorn Museum and Sculpture
Garden, Smithsonian Institution, Washington, D.C.

174. Naton, Abraham
Fisherman, 1951
Oil on canvas, 47⅝ x 38⅛ in. (121 x 97 cm.)
Collection The Tel Aviv Museum of Art, Israel

175. Nevelson, Louise *
Homage to Six Million I, 1964
Painted wood, 108 x 216 in. (2,74 x 5,48 cm.)
Collection Department of Art, Brown University,
Providence, Rhode Island,
Gift of The Albert A. List Family Collection

176. Newman, Barnett *
Joshua, 1950
Oil on canvas, 36 x 25 in. (91.4 x 63.5 cm.)
Collection Mrs. Samuel Weiner, New York

177. Ofek, Abraham
Conversation, 1970
Oil on canvas, 52 x 40 in. (132 x 101.5 cm.)
Lent by the artist, Jerusalem

178. Ofek, Abraham
The Synagogue, 1971
Oil on canvas, 40 x 52 in. (101.5 x 132 cm.)
Lent by the artist, Jerusalem

179. Ofek, Abraham *
Villagers, 1969
Oil on canvas, 64 x 52 in. (162.5 x 132 cm.)
Lent by the artist, Jerusalem

180. Pann, Abel
Expulsion, n.d.
Gouache on canvas, 14 x 9 in. (35.5 x 22.8 cm.)
Collection Mrs. Olga Bineth, Jerusalem

181. Paris, Harold
Kaddish for the Little Children (Europe 1935-1945), 1967-75
Environment, mixed media, 28 x 17 x 8 ft. (8,53 x 5,18 x
2,43 m.)
Lent by the artist, Oakland, California

182. Paris, Harold
*Soul Series 1974—"Moment in M" Munich Olympics
September 5, 1973 (Version II)*, 1974
Cast silicone and colorants, 10 x 8 in. (25.4 x 20.3 cm.)
Lent by the artist, Oakland, California

183. Paris, Harold *
Soul Series 1975—All that Remains (in memory of the Six
Million), 1975
Cast silicone and colorants, 12½ x 10 in. (31.7 x 25.4
cm.)
Lent by the artist, Oakland, California

184. Pascin, Jules
The Brunette (La Brune), 1921
Oil on canvas, 32 x 25⅝ in. (80.7 x 64.7 cm.)
Collection The Hirshhorn Museum and Sculpture
Garden, Smithsonian Institution, Washington, D.C.

185. Pasternak, Leonid *
Max Lieberman Opening Exhibition of the Academy in Berlin,
1930
Oil on canvas, 38⅝ x 30⅜ in. (98 x 77 cm.)
Collection The Tel Aviv Museum of Art

186. Pasternak, Leonid
Portrait of Saul Tchernichowsky, 1923
Oil on canvas, 27½ x 22¾ in. (70 x 58 cm.)
Collection The Tel Aviv Museum of Art

187. Pevsner, Antoine
Twinned Column (Colonne Jumelée), 1947
Bronze, 40½ x 14 x 14 in. (102.8 x 35.5 x 35.5 cm.)
Collection The Solomon R. Guggenheim Museum, New
York

188. Rapoport, Nathan
Exodus, 1971
Bronze, 14 x 22 x 14 in. (35.5 x 55.8 x 35.5 cm.)
Lent by the artist, New York

189. Rapoport, Nathan
Jacob Wrestling with the Angel, 1962
Bronze with marble base, 13 x 12 x 5½ in. (33 x 30 x 13.9
cm.)
Lent by the artist, New York

190. Rattner, Abraham
Ezekial's Valley of the Dried Bones, 1963
Oil on canvas, 77½ x 51 in. (196.8 x 129.5 cm.)
Lent by Kennedy Galleries, Inc., New York

191. Rattner, Abraham
Six Million #2, 1963
Oil on canvas, 45 x 58 in. (114.3 x 147.3 cm.)
Lent by Kennedy Galleries, Inc., New York

192. Rattner, Abraham
Song of Liberation, 1945
Oil on canvas, 31¾ x 39½ in. (80.6 x 100.3 cm.)
Lent by Kennedy Galleries, Inc., New York

193. Reder, Bernard
Hasid with Bird, 1955
Bronze, 25½ in. high (64.1 cm.)
Collection Dr. Morton Hecht, La Jolla, California

194. Reder, Bernard
Organ Player, 1959
Bronze, 15½ x 13½ x 18 in. (39.3 x 34.2 x 45.7 cm.)
Collection Mrs. Otto L. Spaeth, New York

195. Ritterband, Olly
Auschwitz — In the Hut
Oil on canvas, 13¼ x 16½ in. (33.6 x 41.9 cm.)
Collection The Museum of Denmark's Fight for
Freedom, Copenhagen

196. Rivers, Larry
Bar Mitzvah Photograph Portrait, 1961
Oil on canvas, 72 x 60 in. (182.8 x 152.4 cm.)
Collection George A. Schneider, New York

197. Rothko, Mark
Entombment I, 1946
Gouache on paper, 20⅜ x 25¾ in. (52 x 65.5 cm.)
Lent by the Whitney Museum of American Art,
New York

198. Rothko, Mark
Untitled, 1968
Tempera on paper, 40¼ x 25¾ in. (100.5 x 65.5 cm.)
Collection Clinton Wilder, New York

199. Rubin, Reuven *
Arab Fisherman, 1928
Oil on canvas, 30 x 24 in. (76.2 x 60 cm.)
Collection Mr. and Mrs. Harold J. Ruttenberg,
Pittsburgh and Jerusalem

200. Rubin, Reuven
The Road to Bethlehem, 1939
Oil on canvas, 21½ x 28¾ in. (54.6 x 73 cm.)
Collection Philadelphia Museum of Art,
The Louis E. Stern Collection

201. Rubin, Reuven
Self Portrait, 1924
Oil on masonite, 35¾ x 25¼ in. (90 x 64.1 cm.)
Collection Nechemia Glezer, New York

202. Rubin, Reuven
Silent Prayer, 1950
Oil on canvas, 32 x 23¾ in. (81.2 x 60.3 cm.)
Collection The Jewish Museum, New York,
Gift of Richard Zeisler

203. Rubin, Reuven
Woman Preparing for the Sabbath, 1920-21
Oil on canvas, 32 x 44½ in. (81.2 x 113 cm.)
Collection Mr. and Mrs. Jack Resnick, New York

204. Ryback, Issachar
Gifts to the Bride, n.d.
Oil on canvas, 21⅝ x 18⅛ in. (55 x 46 cm.)
Collection The Tel Aviv Museum of Art

205. Ryback, Issachar *
The Old Synagogue, 1917
Oil on canvas, 57½ x 38⅛ in. (146 x 97 cm.)
Colleetion The Tel Aviv Museum of Art

206. Ryback, Issachar
Succoth Still Life, 1925
Oil and collage on canvas, 37 x 23⅝ in. (94 x 60 cm.)
Collection The Israel Museum, Jerusalem

207. Ryback, Issachar
The Synagogue of Chiklov, n.d.
Oil on canvas, 28¾ x 21¼ in. (73 x 54 cm.)
Collection The Tel Aviv Museum of Art

208. Seba, Shalom *
Shearing of Sheep, 1947
Oil on perspex, 18⅞ x 24¾ in. (48 x 63 cm.)
Collection The Tel Aviv Museum of Art

209. Segall, Lasar
Barbed Wire, 1955-56
Oil on canvas, 20½ x 28¼ in. (52 x 71.7 cm.)
Collection Associação Museu Lasar Segall, São Paulo,
Brazil

210. Segall, Lasar
Concentration Camp, 1945
Oil on canvas, 32 x 72¾ in. (81.2 x 184.7 cm.)
Collection Associação Museu Lasar Segall, São Paulo,
Brazil

211. Segall, Lasar
The Condemned, 1950-51
Oil on canvas, 63¾ x 79 in. (161.5 x 200 cm.)
Collection Associação Museu Lasar Segall, São Paulo,
Brazil

212. Segall, Lasar
Emigrant Series, 1928-30
Etching
    a. 8¾ x 10¼ in. (22.2 x 26 cm.)
    b. 11¾ x 14½ in. (29.2 x 36.8 cm.)
    c. 11 x 13 in. (27.9 x 33 cm.)
    d. 11 x 13¾ in. (27.9 x 35 cm.)
Collection Associação Museu Lasar Segall, São Paulo,
Brazil

213. Segall, Lasar *
Emigrant Ship, 1939-41
Oil on canvas, 7 ft. 6 in. x 9 ft. (2,30 x 2,75 m.)
Collection Associação Museu Lasar Segall, São Paulo,
Brazil

214. Segall, Lasar
Exodus, ca. 1940
Oil on canvas, 52 x 54 in. (132 x 137.1 cm.)
Collection The Jewish Museum, New York,
Gift of Messrs. James N. Rosenberg and George Bocker,
in memory of Felix M. Warburg

215. Segall, Lasar
Vision of War, 1940-43
Watercolor, 6 x 7¾ in. (15.2 x 19.6 cm.)
Collection Associação Museu Lasar Segall, São Paulo,
Brazil

216. Seligman, Kurt
Sabbath Phantoms–Mythomonia, n.d.
Oil on canvas, 37 x 50¼ in. (93.9 x 127.6 cm.)
Collection Harold Diamond, New York

217. Shahn, Ben *
East Side Soap Box, 1936
Gouache, 17½ x 11¼ in. (44.4 x 28.5 cm.)
Private collection

218. Shahn, Ben *
Identity, 1968
Mixed media on paper, 40 x 27½ in. (101.5 x 69.8 cm.)
Lent by Kennedy Galleries, Inc., New York

219. Shahn, Ben
Jeremiah 9:1, 1964
Watercolor and gouache, 27 x 21 in. (68.5 x 53.3 cm.)
Collection Mr. and Mrs. Jacob Schulman, Gloversville,
New York

220. Shahn, Ben
Labori and Picquart (from *Dreyfus Series),* 1930
Watercolor, 14½ x 10 in. (36.8 x 25.4 cm.)
Lent by Kennedy Galleries, Inc., New York

221. Shahn, Ben
Georges Picquart (from *Dreyfus Series),* 1930
Watercolor, 14¾ x 10 in. (37.4 x 25.4 cm.)
Lent by Kennedy Galleries, Inc., New York

222. Shahn, Ben
Ram's Horn and Menorah, 1958
Tempera, 27¼ x 16 in. (69.2 x 40.6 cm.)
Collection Mr. and Mrs. Jacob Schulman, Gloversville,
New York

223. Simon, Johanon
In the Shower, 1952
Oil on canvas, 37 x 25⅛ in. (94 x 64 cm.)
Collection The Tel Aviv Museum of Art

224. Simon, Johanon
Sabbath in the Kibbutz, n.d.
Oil on canvas, 25¾ x 19¾ in. (65.5 x 50 cm.)
Collection The Tel Aviv Museum of Art

225. Simon, Johanon
Work, ca. 1945
Oil on canvas, 31½ x 25⅝ in. (80 x 65 cm.)
Collection Menachem Bader, Kibbutz Mizra, Israel

226. Simon, Johanon *
Sabbath in the Kibbutz, 1950
Oil on canvas, 25 x 19½ in. (63.5 x 49.5 cm.)
Collection Tina and Shelomo Ben–Israel, Hollis, New
York

227. Siporin, Mitchell *
Endless Voyage, 1946
Oil on canvas, 34½ x 39⅜ in. (87.6 x 99.5 cm.)
Collection Museum of Art, University of Iowa, Iowa
City

228. Soutine, Chaim
Dead Fowl, 1924
Oil on canvas, 43½ x 32 in. (110.4 x 81.2 cm.)
Collection The Museum of Modern Art, New York,
Gift of Mr. and Mrs. Justin K. Thannhauser, 1958

229. Soutine, Chaim
Fish and Tomatoes, 1925
Oil on canvas, 25¼ x 33½ in. (64.1 x 85 cm.)
Collection Mr. and Mrs. Jack I. Poses, New York

230. Soutine, Chaim
Portrait of Madeleine Castaing, 1928
Oil on canvas, 39⅜ x 28⅞ in. (99.5 x 73.1 cm.)
Lent by The Metropolitan Museum of Art, New York,
Bequest of Miss Adelaide Milton de Groot, (1876-1967),
1967

231. Soutine, Chaim *
Landscape at Céret, 1919
Oil on canvas, 28¼ x 20¾ in. (71.7 x 52.7 cm.)
Collection Mr. and Mrs. Nathan Cummings, New York

232. Soutine, Chaim *
Woman in Profile, 1937
Oil on canvas, 18½ x 11 in. (46.9 x 27.9 cm.)
Collection The Phillips Collection, Washington, D.C.

233. Soutine, Chaim
Woman in Red, 1927-30
Oil on cardboard, 25½ x 19¾ in. (64.7 x 50.1 cm.)
Collection Philadelphia Museum of Art,
The Louis E. Stern Collection

234. Soutine, Chaim
Young Girl at a Fence, (La Fillette à la barrière), ca. 1942
Oil on canvas, 33 x 25½ in. (83.8 x 64.7 cm.)
Collection Mr. and Mrs. Nathan Cummings, New York

235. Soyer, Isaac
Employment Agency, 1937
Oil on canvas, 34¼ x 45 in. (87 x 114.2 cm.)
Lent by the Whitney Museum of American Art, New
York

236. Soyer, Moses
The Lover of Books, 1934
Oil on canvas, 42 x 23½ in. (106.6 x 59.6 cm.)
Collection The Jewish Museum, New York,
Gift of Mrs. Moses Soyer

237. Soyer, Moses
Old Man in Scull Cap, after 1913
Oil on canvas, 29¾ x 21½ in. (75.5 x 54.6 cm.)
Collection The Jewish Museum, New York,
Gift of Mr. Henry Margoshes

238. Soyer, Raphael *
Artist's Parents, 1932
Oil on canvas, 28 x 30 in. (71.1 x 76.2 cm.)
Lent by the artist, New York

239. Soyer, Raphael
Dancing Lesson, 1926
Oil on canvas, 24 x 20 in. (60.9 x 50.8 cm.)
Collection Mr. and Mrs. Chaim Gross, New York

240. Soyer, Raphael
East Side Street, 1930
Oil on canvas, 20 x 24 in. (50.8 x 60.9 cm.)
Lent by the artist, New York

241. Soyer, Raphael
Seamstress, 1956-60
Oil on canvas, 30 x 24⅛ in. (76.2 x 61.3 cm.)
Collection The Museum of Modern Art, New York,
Gift of Mr. and Mrs. Sidney Elliott Cohn, 1961

242. Soyer, Raphael
The Subway, 1928
Oil on canvas, 27½ x 27½ in. (69.8 x 69.8 cm.)
Lent by the artist, New York

243. Steinhardt, Jacob
In the Synagogue, 1923
Ink and wash, 4½ x 7 in. (11.4 x 17.7 cm.)
Collection Mrs. Olga Bineth, Jerusalem

244. Struck, Herman
Separation (Havdalah), 1902
Etching, 10 x 15¾ in. (25.4 x 40 cm.)
Collection The Jewish Museum, New York,
In honor of the memory of Mrs. Tillie E. Hyman
and Dr. and Mrs. Harold K. Addelstein

245. Ticho, Anna
After the War, 1967
Charcoal and crayon on paper, 22 x 28 in.
(55.8 x 71.1 cm.)
Collection Mr. and Mrs. Herman Spertus, Glencoe,
Illinois

246. Ticho, Anna
Jerusalem Hills, 1963
Charcoal on paper, 20⅜ x 27½ in. (51.3 x 69.8 cm.)
Collection The Museum of Modern Art, New York

247. Ticho, Anna
Jerusalem Hills, n.d.
Charcoal on paper
Collection The Tel Aviv Museum of Art

248. Tofel, Jennings
Family Reunion, 1928
Oil on canvas, 18⅛ x 21¾ in. (46.2 x 55.2 cm.)
Collection The Hirshhorn Museum and Sculpture
Garden, Smithsonian Institution, Washington, D. C.

249. Tumarkin, Igael
Homage to Hieronimus Bosch, 1966-67
Bronze, 77 x 27½ x 33 in. (195.5 x 69.8 x 83.8 cm.)
Lent by the artist, New York

250. Walkowitz, Abraham *
East Side Crowd, 1903
Ink on paper, 10 x 7 in. (25.4 x 17.7 cm.)
Collection Mr. and Mrs. H. Lawrence Herring, New
York

251. Weber, Max
Adoration of the Moon, 1944
Oil on canvas, 48 x 32 in. (121.9 x 81.2 cm.)
Lent by the Whitney Museum of American Art, New
York

252. Weber, Max
Balcony, 1939
Oil on canvas, 21 x 26 in. (53.3 x 66 cm.)
Collection Mr. and Mrs. Jacob Schulman, Gloversville,
New York

253. Weber, Max *
The Talmudists, 1934
Oil on canvas, 50 x 33¾ in. (127 x 85.8 cm.)
Collection The Jewish Museum, New York

254. Weinberg, Elbert
Abraham, Isaac, and the Angel #1, 1960
Bronze, 18 x 17 x 17 in. (45.7 x 43.1 x 43.1 cm.)
Collection Mr. and Mrs. Jacob Schulman, Gloversville,
New York

255. Weinberg, Elbert
Ark, 1969
Bronze, 13 x 12 x 8 in. (33 x 30.4 x 20.3 cm.)
Collection Mr. and Mrs. Jacob Schulman, Gloversville,
New York

256. Weinberg, Elbert
Jacob Wrestling with the Angel, 1969
Bronze, 10¼ x 7 x 4½ in. (26 x 17.7 x 11.4 cm.)
Collection Mr. and Mrs. Jacob Schulman, Gloversville,
New York

257. Weinberg, Elbert
The Procession (3 parts), 1957
Bronze,
      a. 105 in. high (266.5 cm.)
      b. 70 in. high (178 cm.)
      c. 94 in. high (238.6 cm.)
Collection The Jewish Museum, New York
Gift of The Albert A. List Family and Friends

258. Werkman, Hendrik
Hassidic Legends, n.d.
Stencil on board, 20⅛ x 13 in. (51.1 x 32.9 cm.)
Collection Stedelijk Museum, Amsterdam

259. Werkman, Hendrik
Hassidic Legends (from *Revelations*), n.d.
Stencil on board, 20⅛ x 13 in. (51.2 x 32.9 cm.)
Collection Stedelijk Museum, Amsterdam

260. Werkman, Hendrik
Hassidic Legends (from *The Triple Laughter*), n.d.
Stencil on board, 20⅛ x 13 in. (51.2 x 32.8 cm.)
Collection Stedelijk Museum, Amsterdam

261. Zaritsky, Joseph
Safed View, ca. 1924
Watercolor over graphite, 24¾ x 24 in. (63 x 61 cm.)
Collection The Israel Museum, Jerusalem

262. Zorach, William
Man of Judah, n.d.
Granite, 17 in. high (43 cm.)
Collection The Zorach Children, Brooklyn

263. Zucker, Jacques
Eviction, 1933
Oil on canvas, 34 x 36 in. (86.3 x 91.4 cm.)
Lent by the artist, New York

264. Zucker, Jacques
Synagogue of the Cabala, 1950
Oil on canvas, 30 x 36 in. (76.2 x 91.4 cm.)
Lent by the artist, New York

232. Chaim Soutine. *Woman in Profile.* 1937. Oil on canvas. 18½ x 11 in. Collection The Phillips Collection, Washington, D.C.

144. Jacques Lipchitz. *Miracle II.* 1947. Bronze. 30½ x 14 in. Collection The Jewish Museum, New York. Gift of Karl Nathan.

Artists' Biographies

Alfred Aberdam (1894–1963)
B. in Lvov, Poland. Aberdam studied painting at the Munich Academy (1913–14). In the Austrian Army during the War, he was wounded on the Russian front and captured. Aberdam stayed in Russia, where he participated in the Revolution and when the Red Army conquered Irkutzk he was appointed Director of the local museum. Returning to Europe in 1920, he studied at the Cracow Academy and then in Berlin with Archipenko. In Paris after 1923, Aberdam had several one-man exhibitions. He remained in Paris in hiding during the Nazi occupation. In 1949 and 1952 he visited Israel and exhibited in Tel Aviv, Haifa, and Jerusalem.

Aronson, C., *Art Polonais Moderne*, Paris, 1929.

Jankel Adler (1895–1949)
B. in Lodz, Poland. Adler lived in Germany from 1913 to 1933. Adler had trained in Poland to be a goldsmith and engraver. His international reputation was established in 1926 with his decoration of the Düsseldorf Planetarium. Fleeing Germany in 1933, Adler lived precariously in various European capitals, finally settling in England in 1941. Adler's work has been exhibited extensively throughout Europe— at the Palais des Beaux-Arts, Brussels (1946), and at Gimpel Fils Gallery in London and in Paris. The Arts Council of Great Britain held a memorial exhibition of his work in 1951.

Klapheck, A., *Jankel Adler*, Recklinghausen, 1966.

Yaacov Agam (1928–)
B. in Rishon-le-Zion, Israel. Agam attended Bezalel School of Arts and Crafts, Jerusalem (1947–49) and the School of Arts and Crafts, Zurich (1949–51). Agam, an innovator in kinetic art, produced variable paintings and sculptures that often use acoustic and light effects. His first of many one-man exhibitions was in 1953 at the Craven Gallery, Paris. He has also had a retrospective at The Tel Aviv Museum of Art (1959) and he was awarded the Grand Prix at the São Paulo Biennale (1963). An experimenter with art theories and visual communication, Agam is also noted for his decoration of the anteroom of the Elysée Palace, Paris (1972) and for his outdoor sculpture. He currently lives in Paris.

Gamzu, H. and Agam, Y., *Transformables*, New York, 1971.

Mordecai Ardon (1896–)
B. in Tuchow, Poland. At the Bauhaus in Germany from 1920 to 1925, Ardon studied with Kandinsky, Klee, Itten, and Feininger. He is known as an art educator as well as a painter of Jewish cultural themes. In Jerusalem Ardon taught at the Bezalel School of Arts and Crafts from 1935 to 1952, becoming its Director in 1940. In 1952 he became Art Advisor to the Israel Ministry of Education. His international reputation has been confirmed in numerous one-man shows, including those held at The Jewish Museum, New York (1948) and the Stedelijk Museum, Amsterdam (1960–61) and at The Tel Aviv Museum of Art (1963).

Grohmann, W., *Ardon*, New York, 1967.

Boris Aronson (1900–)
B. in Kiev. Before emigrating to New York in 1923, Aronson studied at the State Art School of Kiev; the School of Theatre, Kiev; in Berlin with Herman Struck; and in Paris. Known primarily as a theatrical stage designer, Aronson's first one-man show of designs, models, and costume drawings was at the Anderson Galleries, New York (1927). Subsequent major exhibitions have been held at J. B. Neumann's Art Circle, New York (1931, 1940); The Museum of Modern Art, New York (1947); and Saidenberg Gallery, New York (1962). Aronson, currently living in New York, was the recipient of a Guggenheim Grant (1950).

George, W., *Boris Aronson et l'art du theatre*, Paris, 1928.

David Aronson (1923–)
B. in Lithuania. Aronson emigrated to New England prior to World War II. Educated at

Boston Museum School, he is currently Professor of art at Boston University. His work has been exhibited in New York at Nordness Gallery (1960, 1963, 1969) and Danenberg Gallery (1969, 1972). In various media, sculptural relief, painting and drawing, Aronson has participated in group exhibitions in New York at The Museum of Modern Art and the Whitney Museum of American Art. His most important honors include a Guggenheim Fellowship (1960) and Purchase Prize, Pennsylvania Academy of Fine Arts (1969). Aronson is noted for his intense expression of Old and New Testament themes.

Danenberg Gallery, *David Aronson*, New York, 1972.

Samuel Bak (1933-   )

B. in Vilna, Lithuania. Corralled into the Vilna Ghetto in 1940, Bak and his mother escaped only to be recaptured. Two years later Bak had his first exhibition of drawings there. His formal art education included classes at the Vilna Academy (1945); with Professor Blocherer in Munich (1946-48); at the Bezalel School of Arts and Crafts, Jerusalem (1952-53), and at the Beaux Arts Atelier, Paris (1956-59). Since his first one-man exhibition at Galleria Schneider, Rome (1959), Bak has had several shows—at The Tel Aviv Museum of Art, and the Bezalel National Museum, Jerusalem, both in 1963, the Bronfman Cultural Center, Montreal (1970) and Aberbach Fine Art, New York (1974). Drawing on Surrealism of Dali and Magritte, Bak continues to render his fantastic—sometimes frightening—vision as if belonging to everyday reality. Bak currently lives in New York.

Nagano, P. *Bak, Paintings of the Last Decade*, New York, 1971.

Max Band (1900-1974)

B. in Naumestis, Lithuania. Band studied painting in Berlin from 1920 to 1922 and lived in Paris until 1940 when he was forced to flee the Nazis. Band settled in California where he continued to paint within the tradition of the School of Paris. His work includes many Biblical themes; Band is also known for his portraits. From 1964 Band was the first Artist-in-Residence of the University of Judaism, School of Fine Arts, Los Angeles which he helped to found in 1954. D. in California.

Millier, A., *The Art of Max Band*, Los Angeles, 1945.

Leonard Baskin (1922-   )

B. in New Jersey. Baskin grew up in Brooklyn where as the son of an orthodox rabbi he was sent to a yeshiva. He studied at the Educational Alliance Art School, New York; New York University; and at Yale University where he

founded the Gehanna Press in 1942. Of the many one-man exhibitions of his evocative figurative sculpture and graphics, the most significant were held by The Museum of Modern Art, New York (1962), and the Borgenicht Gallery (1953-1969). Baskin has received a Tiffany Fellowship (1947) and a Guggenheim Fellowship (1953). His graphics were included in the São Paulo Biennale (1961) and the Venice Biennale (1968). He currently teaches at Smith College, Northampton, Massachusetts where he has been on the faculty since 1953.

Kennedy Galleries, *Leonard Baskin: Recent Sculpture and Drawing*, New York, 1975.

Max Beckmann (1884-1950)

B. in Leipzig, Germany. Beckmann's art education included study at the Weimar Art School in 1899 and a trip to Paris (1903-04). Settling in Berlin in 1906, Beckmann was an immediate success as a member of the Berlin Secession. His characteristic deformed expressionist imagery, termed "the new objectivity", was not fully developed until after his service in the Army Medical Corps (1914-15). Beckmann taught art at the Frankfurt Art School (1915-33) when he was dismissed by the Nazi authorities; at Washington University, St. Louis (1947-49); and at the Brooklyn Museum. His work was exhibited at the German Pavilion in the Venice Biennale (1950). Notable retrospective exhibitions of his work were held at City Art Museum, St. Louis (1948) and The Museum of Modern Art, New York (1964). D. in New York.

Fischer, F., *Max Beckmann*, Munich, 1972.

Ben-Zion (1897-   )

B. in the Ukraine. A painter and a sculptor, Ben-Zion studied in Vienna and came to the United States in 1920. An amateur artist until 1933, Ben-Zion was self-taught. His religious images have been exhibited in group and one-man shows since 1936. His work has been given major retrospectives—The Bezalel National Museum, Jerusalem (1957), The Jewish Museum, New York (1959). Ben-Zion taught painting at Cooper Union, New York (1943-1950). He lives in New York.

Kayser, S., *Ben-Zion*, The Jewish Museum, New York, 1959.

Yosl Bergner (1920-   )

B. in Vienna. Bergner lived in Warsaw until 1937. He is the son of the Yiddish poet and essayist Melech Ravitch. He emigrated to Australia in 1938 where he studied art. During World War II he joined the Australian Army, and later continued his art studies. In 1948 he left Australia to travel and exhibit in Paris, Montreal, and New York. He emigrated to Israel in 1950.

Bergner participated in the Venice Biennale (1956, 1958, 1962), and in the São Paulo Biennale (1957). He exhibited in group shows in London (1958), and Paris (1960). Bergner's current work contains Surrealist and Expressionist characteristics. He has illustrated Kafka, and is also noted as a theatre designer. Bergner lives in Tel Aviv.

Fischer, Y., *Bergner*, Paris, 1971.

Naftali Bezem (1924–)

B. in Essen, Germany. Bezem went to Palestine in 1939 with Youth Aliyah. Bezem studied under Ardon at the Bezalel School of Arts and Crafts, Jerusalem (1943–46). In Paris between 1949 and 1951, Bezem absorbed current European transformations of Surrealism. Bezem has often represented Israel in such exhibitions as the Biennales in Venice and São Paulo. Bezem lives in Jerusalem.

Seitz, W., *Art Israel*, New York, The Museum of Modern Art, 1964.

Hyman Bloom (1913–)

B. in Bounoviski, Lithuania. Bloom soon emigrated to Boston where he studied with Jack Levine under Denman Ross. Like Levine, Bloom worked for the WPA Federal Arts Project in Boston (1933–36). Known for his fantastic and moralistic visions, Bloom usually employs a richly sensuous technique. Currently represented by Dintenfass Gallery, New York, Bloom has had retrospective exhibitions at the Institute of Contemporary Art, Boston (1954) and The University of Connecticut at Storrs (1968).

Institute of Contemporary Arts, Boston, *Hyman Bloom Retrospective*, 1954.

David Bomberg (1890–1958)

B. in Birmingham, England. Bomberg attended evening classes at the City and Guilds (1950–57) and began an apprenticeship in chromo-lithography under Paul Fisher (1907). Breaking his indenture to become an artist, Bomberg attended Walter Sickert's classes at the Westminster School (1908–10) and studied under Wilson Steer, C. W. Nevinson, and Roger Fry at the Slade School of Fine Arts (1911–13). Thus, thoroughly familiar with contemporary innovations—Cubism, Fauvism, Futurism, Vorticism— Bomberg had his first one-man show at the Chenil Gallery, Chelsea in 1914. In 1924 Bomberg travelled to Palestine. Since then, his semi-abstract, richly textured landscapes, flowers and portraits have been shown in such retrospective exhibitions as the Arts Council of Great Britain (1958), and the Tate Gallery, London (1967). D. in London.

Lipke, W., *David Bomberg*, London, 1967.

Jacob Bornfriend (1904–)

B. in Zborow, Czechoslovakia. Bornfriend studied at the Academy of Fine Arts, Prague (1930–35) and fled to England in 1939. Since his first one-man show at the Galerie Fiegl, Prague (1936), Bornfriend has had major shows, notably at the Konsthallen, Upsala (1963), and at Roland, Browse, and Delbanco, London (1950–4, 1959, 1961). Noted for his wall painting, *Jewish Holiday* (1958) at the Jews College, London, Bornfriend usually works with folkloric motifs. He lives in London.

Roland, Browse, and Delbanco, *Jacob Bornfriend: Oil Paintings*, London, 1961.

Erich Brauer (1929–)

B. in Vienna. From 1942 to 1945 Brauer was in a slave labor camp in Vienna. He studied at the Academy of Fine Arts, Vienna (1945–51) and traveled extensively in Europe, Africa, Israel and the United States. Included in international group exhibitions, Brauer has had one-man shows since 1956 at the Neue Galerie, Vienna. Museum retrospectives have been held at The Tel Aviv Museum of Art (1969) and at the Museum des 20. Jahrhunderts, Vienna (1971). Known as a musician, stage designer, filmmaker, printmaker and painter, Brauer explores spiritual and psychological themes, relying on imaginative interpretations. Brauer lives and works in Paris, Vienna, and Ein Hod, Israel.

Brauer, E., *Brauer*, Salzburg, 1973.

Joseph Budko (1888–1940)

B. in Plonsk, Poland. Budko received a traditional Jewish education. He studied art at the Vilna School of Art (1902); in Berlin at the Museum of Arts and Crafts (1910); and graphic art with Herman Struck. Budko emigrated to Palestine in 1933 where he directed the Bezalel School of Arts and Crafts until his death. Strongly identified with the Jewish experience in Eastern Europe, Budko's themes are drawn from memories of childhood, the Synagogue and Jewish history. Budko illustrated prayer books and literary writings of Bialik, Peretz and Sholom Aleichem.

Friedeberger, H., *Joseph Budko*, Berlin, 1929.

Moshe Castel (1909–)

B. in Jerusalem. Castel's father, Rabbi Yehuda Castel, was a renowned Hebraist, Orientalist, artist-designer of synagogue decorations. In 1922 Castel began studying art at the Bezalel School of Arts and Crafts, Jerusalem. In 1927 he went to Paris where he studied at the Académie Julien and at the Academy of Montparnasse. He exhibited in the Salon des Indépendants and in the Salon d'Automne. Returning to Israel in 1940, Castel settled in Safed where he did a series of paintings. He began to use ancient Jewish forms and symbols and Hebrew and Arabic letters. In

1948 he helped to found the New Horizons group, Tel Aviv. From 1951 to 1953 he visited the United States. Castel exhibited murals and stained glass windows at the Biennales of Venice (1949) and São Paulo (1959). Important one-man exhibitions of his work were held at The Tel Aviv Museum of Art (1942); at Galerie K. Flinker, Paris (1963, 1965); and Lefebre Gallery, New York (1964, 1966, 1969).

Tapie, M. and Sachar, H., *Castel*, Neuchâtel, 1968.

Marc Chagall (1887-)

B. in Vitebsk, Russia. Chagall grew up in an orthodox home in the Jewish quarter. Before leaving for Paris in 1910, Chagall studied painting at the St. Petersburg Academy with Leon Bakst. Living in Paris until 1914, Chagall came under the influence of Cubism and Orphism. He exhibited at the Salon des Indépendants and the Salon d'Automne in 1912. From 1915 to 1922 he lived in Russia, and directed the Vitebsk Academy (1918-20), and was a stage and costume designer (1920-22). In 1923 he moved to Paris. Chagall's characteristic evocative and imaginative style has received international acclaim since his first one-man show in Der Sturm Gallery, Berlin, in 1914. Throughout his career, Chagall has worked in various media, including theatre decorations, book illustrations, stained glass windows, printmaking. Chagall has had many retrospective exhibitions—at The Museum of Modern Art, New York (1946) and the Musée des Arts Decoratifs, Paris (1958). Currently living in Vence, Chagall continues to create visions of concrete and fantastic images.

Meyer, F., *Chagall*, New York, [1963].

Marvin Cherney (1925-1967)

B. in Baltimore, Maryland. Cherney studied at the Maryland Institute of Art, the School of Art Studies, New York, and in France and Italy. Since his first one-man show at AFI Gallery, New York (1953), Cherney exhibited at ACA Gallery, New York (1964, 1966), and at Morgan State College, Philadelphia (1968). Like one of his teachers, Isaac Soyer, Cherney portrays New York City people as soulful and mysterious. D. in New York City.

Wilson, S, *Marvin Cherney*, Philadelphia, Morgan State College, 1968.

Jacob Epstein (1880-1959)

B. in New York. Jacob Epstein studied at the Art Students League (1893-1902). Before moving to London in 1905, he studied in Paris at the Ecole des Beaux-Arts and the Académie Julien. A controversial figure from the beginning of his career, Epstein sculpted monumental, often expressively exaggerated forms. In 1952 he published his autobiography, *Let There Be*

Sculpture. Retrospective exhibitions of his work have been held at the Tate Gallery, London (1952) and at Leicester Galleries, London (1960).

Buckle, R., *Jacob Epstein, Sculptor*, New York, 1963.

Sorel Etrog (1933-)

B. in Jassy, Romania. Etrog emigrated to Israel in 1950 and studied art in Tel Aviv. In 1955 he joined the Ein Hod artists' community, where he developed his mature sculpture style that reflects his preoccupation with primitive art and man in relation to the machine. Recipient of a scholarship to the Brooklyn Museum Art School, New York (1958), he lived in New York for several years before moving to Toronto in 1961. Since his first one-man exhibition at Z.O.A., Tel Aviv (1958), Etrog has had exhibitions at La Strozzina, Palazzo Strozzi, Florence (1968); Hanover Gallery, London (1970); McNay Art Institute, San Antonio (1971). Etrog, who lives in Toronto, represented Canada in the Venice Biennale (1965), and received two commissions for the Canadian Pavilion at Expo 1967.

Withrow, W. *Sorel Etrog; Sculpture*, Toronto, 1967.

Fima (1916-)

B. in China of Russian–Jewish parents. Fima studied Chinese painting and calligraphy and in 1943 taught at the Shanghai Academy. Emigrating to Israel (1949), he worked in Beersheba and Jerusalem until 1961. Fima's painting combines aspects of Chinese calligraphy with those of Abstract Expressionism. Fima has had several one-man exhibitions since his first show in Shanghai in 1947—notably at the Baltimore Museum of Art (1960), The Israel Museum, Jerusalem (1970), and The Jewish Museum, New York (1972). Fima currently lives in Paris and Jerusalem.

Goodman, S. T. *Fima*, New York, The Jewish Museum, 1972.

Naum Gabo (1890-)

B. Naum Pevsner in Briansk, Russia. Gabo is the brother of Antoine Pevsner. In 1910 he entered the University of Munich to study medicine and engineering, and he also attended Wölfflin's lectures. Becoming increasingly interested in art, Gabo traveled to Paris (1912-14) where he became familiar with Cubism and Orphism— determinants of his mature style. At the beginning of World War I he traveled to Oslo via Copenhagen, and in 1915 he made his first construction, signed Gabo. Returning to Russia (1917-22) he and his brother issued the *Realist Manifesto*—a proclamation of the Constructivist program in 1920. In Berlin from 1922 to 1932, Gabo propagated Constructivist ideas through international exhibitions of his work, lectures (at the Bauhaus), and participation in the *Abstraction—Création* group. Before settling permanently in the United States in 1952, he worked in England with the *Circle* group. His monumental work at Rockefeller Plaza, New York (1956), and the Rotterdam Construction, Rotterdam (1957) extends previous experiments combining light, space, and time. Major exhibitions of his work have been held at The Museum of Modern Art, New York (1948), the Tate Gallery, London (1965), and Kunsthaus, Zurich (1965). Gabo lives in Middlebury, Connecticut.

De la Motte, M., *Naum Gabo*, Hanover, 1971.

Adolph Gottlieb (1903–1971)

B. in New York. A student at the Art Students League in New York, Gottlieb worked under John Sloan and Robert Henri in 1920. Gottlieb also studied at the Académie de la Grande Chaumière, Paris (1921—23) and at the Parsons School of Design in New York (1923). Gottlieb worked with the WPA Federal Arts Project (1936). Identified with the color field painters of the Abstract Expressionists, Gottlieb developed his characteristic pictographs in the early forties. Since his first one-man show in New York at Dudensing Gallery (1930), Gottlieb has been honored at numerous retrospectives in New York—at The Jewish Museum (1957), The Solomon R. Guggenheim Museum and the Whitney Museum of American Art (1967). He received commissions to decorate synagogues— Park Avenue Synagogue, New York, and Congregation Israel, Milburn, New Jersey. D. in New York.

Doty, R. and Waldman, D., *Adolph Gottlieb*, New York, 1968.

Leopold Gottlieb (1883–1934)

B. in Galicia, Poland. The younger brother of the well-known painter Moritz, Gottlieb studied at the Academy of Art in Cracow and continued his studies in travel to Munich, Vienna, and finally settled in Paris. He showed his Expressionist portraits at the Salon d' Automne (1908–13) and Salon des Indépendants. During World War I he joined the Polish Legion and described the war in numerous paintings. Gottlieb returned to Paris in 1929, where he lived until his death.

Salmon, A, *Leopold Gottlieb*, Paris, 1927.

William Gropper (1897—   )

B. in New York. Gropper studied art at the National Academy of Design and the School of Fine and Applied Art, New York. Like other social realists, Gropper was a staff member of several New York newspapers and contributed illustrations and cartoons to various periodicals in the 1920s and 1930s. He traveled to the Soviet Union with Theodore Dreiser and Sinclair Lewis in 1927. Gropper received a Guggenheim Fellowship in 1939. Retrospectives of his murals,

graphics and paintings have been held at Lowe Art Museum, University of Miami (1968), and the ACA Gallery, New York (1971–72).

Freundlich, A., *William Gropper*, Los Angeles, 1968.

Chaim Gross (1904—   )

B. in Galicia, Austria. Gross studied in Budapest and Vienna. After emigrating to New York (1921), he studied at the Educational Alliance Art School, New York and at the Art Students League of New York. Early in the 1930s he exhibited at galleries in New York. From 1933 to 1935 he worked for the WPA Federal Arts Project, Sculpture Division, New York. He was included in the American National Exhibition in Sokolski Park, Moscow (1959) and showed at the Whitney Museum of American Art, New York (1959). Living in New York City, Gross continues to make figurative sculptures in an Expressionist vein.

Getlen, F., *Chaim Gross*, New York, 1944.

Jose Gurvich (1927–1974)

B. in Lithuania. Gurvich grew up in Uruguay. There, he studied at the Escuela Nacional de Bellas Artes (1942) and in the workshop of Joaquín Torres-García (1945). With other Torres-García students he organized a ceramics workshop and published an art review *Escuela del Sur* (1952). From 1953 to 1957 Gurvich traveled and studied in Europe and Israel. Returning to Montevideo (1957), he again participated in activities with Torres-García students, teaching at the Taller Torres García. From 1957 Gurvich has exhibited in Uruguay, at Galerias Amigos del Arte, Arte Bella, Americana. Other one-man shows were at the Museo Nacional de Bellas Artes, Montevideo (1967), and at the Museo Municipal de Bellas Artes, Buenos Aires (1970). Gurvich travelled frequently to Israel. He came to New York in 1973, where he died.

Correspondence with the artist.

Minna Harkavy (1895-   )

B. in Estonia. After her emigration to New York, Harkavy's art education included classes at the Art Students League, New York and frequent travel and study in Europe. In Parish she worked under Antoine Bourdelle. A figurative expressionist sculptor, Harkavy favors a restrained statement. Her honors include an American Academy of Arts and Letters Grant (1959) and a Medal of Honor from the National Association of Women Artists (1962). Harkavy has exhibited in the United States, Europe and Israel; she has had a one-woman exhibition at Rhode Island School of Design Museum of Art, (1956). Harkavy currently lives and works in New York City.

Whitney Museum of American Art, New York, Artist File.

Josef Herman (1911–   )
B. in Warsaw. From 1930 to 1932 Herman studied at the Warsaw School of Art, and in 1932 he had his first exhibition in Warsaw. He emigrated to Belgium in 1938 and escaped to London in 1940. His subject matter is largely drawn from a small Welsh mining village, Ystradgynlair, where he lived from 1944 to 1953. While his early works are expressionist reflections of ghetto life, his mature and current works are universal statements about the dignity of labor. Widely traveled and known throughout Europe and Israel, Herman has had retrospectives at Whitechapel Art Gallery, London (1956) and at the Glynn Vivian Art Gallery, Swansea (1963). Herman has lived in London since 1953.

Mullins, E, *Josef Herman*, London, 1967.

Samuel Hirszenberg (1865–1908)
B. in Lodz, Poland. Hirszenberg studied in Cracow, Munich, and Paris. In 1907 he went to Jerusalem. Hirszenberg's genre compositions, based on Jewish contemporary and historical events, were popular in Poland during his lifetime. He participated in international exhibitions, notably at the Munich Succession (1891, 1895, 1896), in Berlin (1894, 1895, 1906), and at the Paris Salon (1905, 1906, 1907, 1911). D. in Jerusalem.

Naphtalie, B, *Samuel Hirszenberg*, Berlin, 1929.

Fritz Hundertwasser (1928–   )
B. in Vienna. Hundertwasser studied at the Vienna Academy (1948) and traveled to Tuscany, Paris, Morocco, and Tunisia. His current abstract–decorative style reveals a wide range of influences including Viennese Jugendstil and Expressionism, Oriental miniatures, and Renaissance art. Although Hundertwasser is widely recognized today, his first exhibition at the Art Club, Vienna (1952) drew scandalous critical and public reactions. His honors include the Prix du Syndicat d'Initiative at the Premiére Bordeaux (France) Biennale (1957). He has had retrospectives at the Moderne Museet, Stockholm (1965) and at the University Art Museum, Berkeley (1968).

Chipp, H. and Richardson, B., *Hundertwasser*, Berkeley, University Art Museum, 1968.

Nathaniel Jacobson (1916–   )
B. in Salem, Massachusetts. Jacobson graduated from the Massachusetts School of Art in 1937 and received his BFA from Yale University in 1941. Since his first one-man show at the Today's Art Gallery, Boston (1945), Jacobson has had one-man shows, notably at the Jerusalem Artists House (1956) and The Jewish Museum, New York (1958). The son of a rabbi, Jacobson visited Israel (1956–58). His interest in Israel and in Biblical themes is reflected in his paintings, murals, mosaics, tapestries, and stained glass decorations. He has received commissions from various Jewish organizations including Temple Israel, Great Neck and Temple Israel, Boston. Jacobson lives in Brookline, Massachusetts.

Correspondence with artist.

Marcel Janco (1895–   )
B. in Bucharest. Completing his training as an architect at the Polytechnique, Zurich (1915), Janco participated in Dada activities. He worked on a Dada magazine, *Zurich* (1919), designed posters and decorations for Cabaret Voltaire, and created abstract relief works. Leaving the group which included Arp and Tzara, he lived in Paris (1921–22). In 1923 he returned to Bucharest as an architect and joined the radical artists' group *Contemporanul*. In 1941 Janco went to Palestine where in 1948 he helped to found New Horizons artists' group, Tel Aviv. In 1953 he founded the artists' community, Ein Hod, Israel. He participated in the Venice Biennale (1952) and in the São Paulo Biennale (1954). In contrast to his early work Janco's later works are landscapes, drawn from Israeli views. Janco lives in Tel Aviv and Ein Hod.

Berckelaers, F. L, [M. Seuphor], *Marcel Janco*, Paris, 1963.

Mervin Jules (1912–   )
B. in Baltimore, Maryland. Jules studied at the Maryland Institute of Fine Arts (1930–33) and at the Art Students League, New York (1934) under Thomas Hart Benton. Since his first one-man show at the Hudson Walker Gallery, New York (1937), Jules' work has been exhibited at ACA Gallery, New York (1941–45, 1947, 1954, 1958) and at the University of California (1949). A social realist, Jules observes and sympathizes with the more common aspects of humanity in his characterizations. He currently lives in New York City where he teaches at City College.

New York Public Library, Art Division, Artist File.

Wolf Kahn (1927–   )
B. in Stuttgart, Germany. Moving to New York City (1940), Kahn attended the High School of Music and Art and then studied with Hans Hofmann (1948–49) and graduated from the University of Chicago (1951). A landscape painter since 1952, Kahn's depiction of specific locations evokes a freshness and authentic sense of place. He was a recipient of a Guggenheim Grant (1966) and he was a Fulbright Fellow to Italy (1963–65). Since his first one-man show at Hansa Gallery, New York (1954), Kahn has had numerous one-man exhibitions at the Borgenicht Gallery, New York and has been included in

group exhibitions at the Whitney Museum of American Art, New York (1958, 1959).

Borgenicht Gallery, New York, Artist Biography.

Luise Kaish (1925–   )
B. in Atlanta, Georgia. Kaish earned her BFA and MFA from Syracuse University (1941–1951) respectively. Kaish studied sculpture with Ivan Mestrovic and her work shows a similar expressiveness. Concerned with the symbolic implications of religious themes, Kaish has received commissions for her synagogue sculpture. Her honors include a Guggenheim Grant (1959) and a Rome Prize Fellowship in Sculpture (1970–72). Major one–woman exhibitions have been held at the Sculpture Center, New York (1955, 1958) and the St. Paul Art Center, Minnesota (1969), and at The Jewish Museum, New York (1973). Kaish currently lives in New York City and shows regularly at Staempfli Galleries. She is married to Morton Kaish, a painter.

Kampf, A., *Luise Kaish*, New York, The Jewish Museum, 1973.

Raffi Kaiser (1931–   )
B. in Jerusalem. Kaiser studied at the Tel Aviv Art Academy; Ecole des Beaux-Arts, Paris; with Paul Colin, stage designer; and at the Accademia di Belle Arti, Florence. Since his first one–man exhibition in Florence (1961), Kaiser has had exhibitions at Gallery 44, Brussels (1968), and at Gordon Gallery, Tel Aviv (1968), and has participated in numerous international group exhibitions such as the Salon d'Automne, Paris (1962), *Five Israeli Artists*, University of Michigan. He lives in Paris where he is represented by Edition d'Art. Kaiser creates landscapes that belong to the dream world.

Correspondence with artist.

Morris Kantor (1890–1974)
B. in Minsk, Russia. Kantor came to New York with his parents in 1911. He studied with Robert Henri and Homer Boss at the Art Students League, New York. Kantor showed regularly with Rehn Gallery, New York (1930–59). Other one–man exhibitions were held at the Bertha Schaefer Gallery, New York (1959, 1962, 1965, 1967, 1971), and Davenport Municipal Art Gallery, Iowa, (1965). He taught painting at The Art Students League and Cooper Union. His work spans the artistic movements from Cubism to Abstract Expressionism. D. in Nyack, New York.

Kantor, M., "Ends and Means, Autobiography", *Magazine of Art* (March 1940), pp. 138–147.

Anatole Kaplan (1902–   )
B. in Rogachev, Byelorussia. Kaplan grew up in the same region as Sholom Aleichem and Marc Chagall. After the 1917 Revolution he moved to Leningrad. In 1927 Kaplan graduated from the Academy of Arts. He became a member of the Artists' Union in 1939. He frequently illustrated the writings of Sholom Aleichem. Closely connected with the tradition of Russian–Jewish folklore, Kaplan has had a one-man exhibition in Jerusalem at the Bezalel National Museum (1961), and in New York at The Jewish Museum (1972). He has shown in group exhibitions in Los Angeles, Dresden, Rome, and Prague. He participated in the Venice Biennale (1966) and Expo (1967) in Montreal. Kaplan lives in Leningrad.

Suris, B., *Anatole Kaplan,* Leningrad, 1970.

Dani Karavan (1930–   )
B. in Tel Aviv. Karavan studied at the Avni Studio of Painting and Sculpture, Tel Aviv, with the Expressionist artist–teachers Yeheskiel Streichman, Avigdor Stematsky, and Mordecai Ardon, and learned fresco and mural techniques at the Accademia di Belle Arti, Florence (1956). Committed to the idea of public art, Karavan received his first mural commission from the Sheraton Hotel, Tel Aviv (1959). Subsequent work includes 30 bas–reliefs for the Tel Aviv Court House (1962–67), bas–relief and carpet for Assembly Hall in The Knesset, Jerusalem (1965–66). Since 1958, Karavan has designed for Israeli and American theatre, opera and ballet companies including The Martha Graham Dance Company. Karavan blends tendencies of modern and ancient art in his varied productions. He lives in Tel Aviv.

Kampf, A, *Dani Karavan*, Firenzi, 1971.

Isidore Kaufmann (1853–1921)
B. in Hungary, Kaufmann soon went to Vienna. Trained as a bankteller Kaufmann began to study art in 1876 in Vienna under J. M. Aigner and J. Trenwald. Known for his depictions of Jewish life, he worked within the realist tradition. His miniatures, highly detailed and richly colored, have won awards in Vienna, Berlin, Munich and Paris. D. in Vienna.

Schwartz, K., *Jewish Artists of the 19th and 20th Centuries*, New York, 1949.

Edward Kienholz (1927–   )
B. in Fairfield, Washington. Kienholz studied at Eastern Washington College of Education. In 1953, he moved to Los Angeles where he founded Now Gallery, with Sydell Studios (1956). After Now Gallery closed (1957), he opened Ferus Gallery, Los Angeles, with Walter Hopps. Since his first one–man show at Café Galleria, Los Angeles (1955), Kienholz has had exhibitions at the Pasadena Art Museum (1961), Los Angeles County Museum of Art (1968), and at the Kunsthaus, Zurich (1971). A Funk artist,

Kienholz creates tableaux or realistic environments that reveal the horrors of everyday existence.

Baumann, F., *Edward Kienholz*, Zurich, Kunsthaus, 1971.

Michael Kiköine (1892-1968)

B. in Gomel, Russia. Kiköine studied at Vilna School of Art; Ecole des Beaux-Arts; Paris, and in the Cormon Atelier, Paris (1913). A *peintre maudit*, Kiköine worked within the *La Ruche* circle that included Chagall, Soutine, Krémègne—all Russian Jews. Following his service for the French Army during World War I, Kiköine began to paint his characteristic portraits of children, exhibited in his first one-man show at the Galerie Licorne, Paris (1919). In 1950 and again in 1953 Kiköine visited Israel, where he had exhibitions in museums in Tel Aviv, Haifa, and Jerusalem. Other exhibitions of his work have been held at Galerie Marcel Bernheim, Paris (1927), Galerie Brummer, New York (1949), Redfern Gallery, London (1955). D. in Paris.

Betlex-Cailler, N., *Kiköine*, Geneva, 1957.

Yeheskel Kirszenbaum (1900-1954)

B. in Staszow, Poland. The son of a rabbinic scholar, Kirzenbaum began his career as a signboard painter for local tradesmen. In 1917 he emigrated to Germany and studied briefly at the Bauhaus in Weimar. He lived in Berlin until 1933 and, under the pseudonym Duvdevani, worked as a newspaper illustrator and cartoonist. Kirzenbaum moved to Paris (1933) and went into hiding during the German occupation. His studio was ransacked; his wife murdered. Kirzenbaum's paintings and etchings are melancholy evocations, synthesizing Eastern European themes in an Expressionist style. D. in Paris.

Waldemar, G., "School of Paris," in *Jewish Art, an illustrated history*, edited by Cecil Roth, New York, 1971, pp. 697-698.

Liliane Klapisch (1933-   )

B. in suburban Paris to Polish emigré parents. Klapisch's family fled Paris during World War II. In 1947 she started to paint, and studied at the Académie Ranson in Montparnasse and in Italy in 1953. Between 1963 and 1968 she exhibited with the abstract painters *Realités Nouvelles* in Paris and in 1966 had a one-woman show at the Galerie La Rone, Paris. From 1958 to 1960 Klapisch lived in Morocco, and between 1962 and 1968 she resided in Paris. In 1968 she went to Israel and settled in Jerusalem where she is represented by Bineth Gallery. Her current work characterizes urban Jerusalem.

Correspondence with artist.

Yehoshua Kovarsky (1907-1967)

B. in Vilna, Lithuania. Sent to Palestine (1924), Kovarsky studied painting with an older Yeminite friend while working on a kibbutz near Jerusalem. Before returning to Vilna in 1928 to attend the Academy of Fine Arts, Kovarsky stayed briefly in Paris, becoming familiar with the modern tradition. From 1935 to 1949 he lived in Israel—first in the artistic community of Safed, then as an art teacher in Zichron Ya'akov. Residing in New York City from 1949, Kovarsky continued to explore kabalistic ideas. After his first one-man show in 1935 at the Vilna Academy, Kovarsky exhibited at The Jewish Museum, New York (1956), the Bezalel National Museum, Jerusalem (1958); and regularly at Poindexter Gallery, New York from 1962 until his death.

Kayser, S., *Yehoshua Kovarsky*, New York, The Jewish Museum, 1956.

Leopold Krakauer (1890-1954)

B. in Vienna. Krakauer trained as an engineer and architect and graduated from the Imperial Academy of Fine Arts, Vienna. In 1929 he went to Palestine and settled in Jerusalem. Since his first one-man show at Steimatzky Gallery, Jerusalem, Krakauer has had numerous exhibitions—notably at The Tel Aviv Museum of Art (1953), Bezalel National Museum, Jerusalem (1954, 1955, 1964), and at the Venice Biennale of 1954 where he represented Israel. The landscape of Jerusalem and its environs is poetically reinterpreted in Krakauer's black chalk drawings. D. in Jerusalem.

Cohen, E, *Krakauer*, Jerusalem, 1974.

Jacob Kramer (1892-1962)

B. in Klintsky, Ukraine. With his family, Kramer emigrated to England and settled in Leeds where he spent most of his life. Encouraged by his father, Max, and his uncle, Sion,—both painters— to become an artist, he attended the Leeds School of Art (1907-11) and the Slade School of Art, London (1912). His intense and simplified expressionist vision is evident in both painting and graphics. Noted as the "Modigliani of Leeds", Kramer has been honored, as an artist and educator, in a retrospective exhibition of his work at the Leeds City Art Gallery, 1960 and in the renaming of the Leeds College of Art in his name.

Kramer, M. ed., *Kramer Memorial Volume*, London, 1969.

Walt Kuhn (1877-1949)

B. in Brooklyn, New York. Kuhn studied at the Polytechnic Institute of Brooklyn (1893), the Académie Colarossi, Paris (1901), and the Bayerische Akademie der Schönen Künste, Munich (1901-03). After extensive travel in

Europe, Kuhn returned to New York and earned his living (1905-14) as a cartoonist for such publications as *Life, Puck,* the *New York Sun,* and the *New York World.* As one of the organizers of the Armory Show and as a teacher and advisor to art collectors, Kuhn, throughout his career, encouraged avant-garde art in America and helped to transmit European innovations to America. Since his first one-man show at the Madison Gallery, New York (1910-11) Kuhn has been honored at numerous exhibitions including at the Columbus Gallery of Fine Arts (1935, 1942); the Durand-Ruel Galleries, New York (1943-46, 1948). D. in White Plains, New York.

Getlein, F., *Walt Kuhn,* New York, 1967.

Issai Kulvianski (1892-1970)
B. in Lithuania. Kulvianski studied in Vilna from 1908 to 1912 (at the High School of Fine Arts); in Berlin briefly in 1912 and again in 1915 following his release from prison camp. A participant in the exuberant cultural life of Berlin in the twenties, Kulvianski encountered a wide range of avant-garde expression. His work in sculpture, painting, and stage design reflects his simultaneous preoccupation with figurative and abstract styles. Fleeing Nazi Berlin in 1933, Kulvianski settled in Palestine, establishing an art school in Tel Aviv. He had his first exhibition at the Steimatzky bookshop in Jerusalem. In 1950 Kulvianski returned to Europe and spent his last years making sculpture in Berlin. Following his death in 1970, he was honored with a retrospective exhibition at the Berlin-West Gallery, Berlin (1974).

Roters, E., *Retrospective-Issai Kulvianski,* Berlin, 1974.

Maurico Lasansky (1914-   )
B. in Buenos Aires. Lasansky's father, a printer from Lithuania, encouraged his study of painting, sculpture, and engraving at the Superior School of Fine Arts, Buenos Aires in 1933. Lasansky worked with Hayter at Atelier 17, New York and studied the print collection at the Metropolitan Museum of Art, New York, and in European museums through Guggenheim Grants (1943, 1944, 1953). Known for his technical facility and experimental approach, Lasansky considers printmaking to be a medium through which thought and emotion can be expressed. Since his first one-man show at Fort General Roca, Negro, Argentina (1935), Lasansky has had retrospective exhibitions at the Muller Gallery, Buenos Aires (1943), the Albright Art Gallery, Buffalo (1959), and the Brooklyn Museum (1961). Lasansky, an American citizen since 1952, teaches graphics at Iowa State University where he was appointed in 1945.

Zigrosser, C., *Maurico Lasansky,* New York, 1960.

Joe Lasker (1919-   )
B. in New York City. Lasker graduated from Cooper Union Art School, New York (1939) and studied at Escuela Universitaria de Bellas Artes, San Miguel de Allende, Mexico. His commissions include murals for Post Offices in Calumet, Michigan and Millbury, Massachusetts, and the Henry Street Settlement Playhouse, New York City. Lasker, represented by Kraushaar Galleries since his first one-man show there in 1951, has also had shows at Philadelphia Alliance (1959) and participated in numerous group exhibitions including group exhibitions at the Whitney Museum of American Art, New York (1947-58) and the National Academy of Design, New York (1947-72). Awarded the Prix de Rome (1950) and a Guggenheim Grant (1954), Lasker lives in South Norwalk, Connecticut.

Kraushaar Galleries, New York, Artist Biography.

Mordecai Levanon (1901-1968)
B. in Hungary. Levanon went to Palestine in 1921 as a pioneer and was a farm worker. From 1922 he studied painting at the Bezalel School of Arts and Crafts, Jerusalem and in 1925 studied with Izhak Frenkel in Tel Aviv. In 1939 he settled in Jerusalem and after 1963 spent time in Safed. He participated in group shows and one-man exhibitions in Israel and Europe, and in the Biennales in Venice and São Paulo. Interested in mysticism, Levanon frequently painted Jerusalem and Safed.

Fischer, Y., "Mordecai Levanon", *Encyclopedia Judaica,* Vol. XI, p. 68.

David Levine (1926-   )
B. in Brooklyn, New York. Levine studied at the Tyler School of Art, Temple University, Philadelphia and at the Hans Hofmann School of Fine Art, New York. He was included in the Whitney Museum of American Art, New York, *Annual,* (1960, 1962). He has taught at the School of Visual Arts, New York and the Brooklyn Museum Art School. His books of drawings include *The Man from M.A.L.I.C.E.* (1966), *Pens and Needles* (1969), and *No Known Survivors* (1970). A Guggenheim Fellow in 1950, Levine is noted for his caricatures and drawings of political and cultural figures. Levine lives in New York.

Levine, D., *No Known Survivors,* Boston, 1970.

Jack Levine (1915-   )
B. in Boston. Levine grew up in the immigrant slums. He studied art with Hyman Bloom under Denman Ross at Harvard. Levine worked with the WPA Project, Easel Division, (1935-1940). Levine's works—figurative, mystic-like narratives—often function as social commentary. He was the recipient of such honors as a Guggenheim Grant (1945, 1947) and a Fulbright

Fellowship (1950). Levine has had retrospectives at the Institute of Contemporary Art, Boston (1952), and the Museum of Art, Ogunquit, Maine (1964). Levine lives in New York.

Getlein, F., *Jack Levine*, New York, 1966.

Isaac Ilyich Levitan (1861-1900)
B. in Wirbatten, Lithuania. Levitan studied at the Moscow School of Art and in 1889 visited Paris where he discovered Corot and the Impressionists. In 1896 Levitan was appointed Professor of landscape painting at The Moscow Academy of Art where he taught until his death. He participated in The World of Art Exhibition in Moscow (1889). Considered a major influence on Russian landscape painting, Levitan helped to bridge the gap between French and Russian art in his melancholic landscape expressions.

Prorokova, S. A., *Levitan*, Russia, 1960.

Max Liebermann (1847-1935)
B. in Berlin. Liebermann spent his student years in Berlin in the studio of the animal painter Karl Steffeck, Weimar, and studied and traveled in Paris and Holland (1872-78). His contact with the Barbizon painters and then the Impressionists formed the basis of his German version of Impressionism. In 1898, he became a founding member and later President of the Berlin Secession; Liebermann is long acknowledged as a leader of German painting. Recent exhibitions of his paintings and graphics have been held at the Ketterer Gallery, Stuttgart (1960), and the Kunsthalle, Hamburg (1968). D. in Berlin.

Scheffler, K., *Max Liebermann*, Munich, 1923.

Ephraim Moses Lilien (1874-1925)
B. in Drohobcz, Poland. Lilien studied at the Academy of Fine Arts in Cracow under Jan Matejko (1890) and at the Academy of Fine Arts, Vienna. In 1894 Lilien went to Munich and contributed to the avant-garde magazine *Die Jugend.* An early and active Zionist, he moved to Berlin in 1898 and became known as a book illustrator and draughtsman. Lilien illustrated an edition of the Bible in the decorative style popular at the time. One of the founders of the Berlin publishing house Jeudischer Verlag, Lilien served as its illustrator, editor, and manager. He helped form the Bezalel School of Arts and Crafts, Jerusalem (1905) where he taught. Since his first one-man show at Bever and Sohn, Leipzig (1900), his work has been known through exhibitions at Heller, Vienna (1909), and publications of his Bible illustrations (1912). D. in Badenweiler.

Brieger, *E.M. Lilien*, Berlin, 1922.

Bronislaw Wojciech Linke (1906-1962)
B. in Tarto, Estonia. Linke studied industrial art in Cracow (1924-6) and fine arts in Warsaw (1927-31). In 1939 he moved to Lvov, earning his living as a graphic artist for magazines. Because he had done caricatures of the Hitler regime, he fled Poland in 1940 and worked in Siberia until his return to Warsaw in 1946. In Warsaw he again contributed to contemporary publications. He went to Paris (1960). Linke is also known for his propaganda posters and graphics shown in exhibitions in Sweden, England and Moscow (1936-8). D. in Warsaw.

National Museum, Warsaw. Artist Biography.

Jacques Lipchitz (1891-1973)
B. Chaim Jacob in Druskienki, Lithuania. Lipchitz moved to Paris (1909) where he studied at the Ecole des Beaux-Arts and the Académie Julien. Early in his career he was friendly with the Parisian avant-garde—Max Jacob, Modigliani, Soutine, Gris, and Picasso. By 1913, under the direct impact of Picasso, he had made Cubist sculpture with his own characteristic expressive content. His first one-man exhibition was at the Léonce Rosenberg Gallery (1920). Fleeing Paris in 1940, he settled in New York City. Lipchitz has been honored with several retrospectives—at The Tel Aviv Museum of Art and the National Gallery, Berlin (1972), and at The Metropolitan Museum of Art, New York (1972). In 1952 Lipchitz became a French citizen. Lipchitz continued to work with universal and humanitarian themes until his death in Capri. He was buried in Jerusalem.

Hammacher, A.M., *Jacques Lipchitz*, New York, 1960.

Seymour Lipton (1903-)
B. in New York. Lipton studied at City College, New York (1922-23) and Columbia University (1923-27). Having had no formal art education, Lipton developed his Abstract Expressionist sculpture primarily on his own. He taught at the New School for Social Research (1940-1964) and was the recipient of a Guggenheim Grant (1960) and a Ford Foundation Grant (1961). Since his first one-man show at A.C.A. Gallery, New York (1938), Lipton has had numerous shows, notably at Betty Parsons Gallery, New York (1948, 1950, 1952, 1954) and The Museum of Modern Art, New York (1956). He was commissioned to do three ritual objects for Temple Israel, Tulsa, Oklahoma (1954) and five for Temple Beth-El, Gary, Indiana (1955). Lipton lives in New York.

Elsen, A., *Seymour Lipton*, New York, 1970.

El Lissitsky (1890-1941)
B. Lazar Markowich in Smolensk, Russia. An architecture student in Darmstadt (1909-14), Lissitsky worked as an architect in Moscow and from 1916 contributed to art exhibitions. With Ryback, Lissitsky explored Jewish folkart on the Dnieper River. In 1919 he met Malevich, whose

Suprematist theories inspired the dynamic spatial construction designs of the *Proun* series. Lissitsky also designed numerous exhibition halls—built in Berlin (1923), in Dresden (1926), and in Hanover (1927-28). In contrast to the Chagall-like illustrated woodcuts (1917-20) are the later works for Constructivist and de Stijl magazines in the twenties, and his propaganda posters of the late thirties. Besides editing and writing for the Constructivist and Dada periodicals, Lissitsky published fiction and nonfiction. Major exhibitions of his work have been held at Grosvenor Gallery, London (1966), and Kestner-Gesellschaft, Hanover (1966). D. in Moscow.

Lissitsky—Kuppers, S., *El Lissitsky,* Dresden, 1967.

Louis Lozowick (1892-1973)

B. in Kiev, Russia, Lozowick emigrated to New York City in 1906. He studied at the National Academy of Design, New York (1912-15), and at Ohio State University, Columbus (1915-18), as well as in Paris and Berlin. Known primarily as an American Precisionist, Lozowick has exhibited prints, drawings, and paintings in numerous one-man and group exhibitions in the United States, Russia, and Europe. Exhibitions have been held at Zabriskie Gallery, New York, Newark Public Library, New Jersey (1969), and the Whitney Museum of American Art, New York (1972). D. in New Jersey.

Solomon, E., *Louis Lozowick,* New York, Whitney Museum of American Art, 1972.

Mané-Katz (1894-1962)

B. in Kremenchug, Ukraine. The son of a synagogue beadle, Mané-Katz received a religious education. From 1914 to 1921, he worked in Russia, painting Cubist-influenced works. Closely associated with the School of Paris, Mané-Katz was in Paris intermittently (1913-21); he became a naturalized French citizen (1927). His extensive travels in the Middle East, including several trips to Israel and the ghettos of Eastern Europe, are reflected in his painting and sculpture. D. in Israel.

Aries, R., *Mané-Katz: The Complete Works,* London, 1970.

Abraham Manievich (1881-1942)

B. in Mstislav, Russia. Manievich studied at the Art School of Kiev, at the Munich Academy of Art, and traveled throughout Europe. His first one-man show was held at the Kiev State Museum of Art in 1910. Highly regarded in Russia, Manievich was elected to a Professorship at the Ukraine Academy of Art, Kiev (1917). Preoccupied with themes of Russian-Jewish life, he worked in an Expressionist vein synthesizing contemporary European developments. After his arrival in America (1922), he had numerous exhibitions: the Art Alliance, Philadelphia (1923); the Baltimore Museum of Art, Baltimore (1928); the French Art Galleries, New York (1943), and The Tel Aviv Museum of Art (1949). D. in New York.

Ein Harod Museum, Israel, Artist File.

Maryan S. Maryan (1927-   )

B. in Poland. Interned in Auschwitz, Maryan arrived in Israel (1947) after two years in displaced persons' camp in Germany. He attended the Bezalel School of Arts and Crafts, Jerusalem where his first one-man show was held at the YMCA in 1949. His socially conscious realist painting and graphics synthesize his personal history in terms of universal concerns. In 1950 Maryan moved to France and studied at the Ecole des Beaux-Arts until 1953. Maryan regularly shows at the Galerie de France, Paris; the Allen Frumkin Gallery, New York and Chicago; and has been included in numerous group shows including *New Realism,* Berlin-Museum (1964); *Human Concern—Personal Torment,* the Whitney Museum of Art, New York (1969); and *Ten Independents,* The Solomon R. Guggenheim Museum, New York (1972). Maryan has lived in New York since 1962.

Allan Frumkin Gallery, New York, Artist Biography.

Sigmund Menkes (1896-   )

B. in Lvov, Poland. Menkes studied at the Higher Institute of Decorative Arts of Lvov (1914), and at the Academy of Cracow (1919); he moved to Paris in 1919, where he lived until his move to the United States in 1936. He is noted for his exuberant painterly treatment of still life and figurative themes. Since his first one-man show in Paris (1922), Menkes has had frequent exhibitions, notably at the Associated American Artists Gallery, New York. Menkes' work is similar to his contemporaries in the School of Paris, and he has received the Corcoran Gold Medal and the first W.A. Clarke Prize (1947). Menkes lives in Riverdale, New York.

New York Public Library, Art Division, Artist File.

Mauricy Minkowsky (1881-1931)

B. in Warsaw, Poland. Deaf and dumb from the age of five, Minkowsky studied in the Academy of Art, Cracow (1900-04). He witnessed the Pogrom in Bialystok, which drastically affected the subject of his works. Never leaving his native Poland, Minkowsky painted Jewish themes—pogroms and the suffering of the Jewish people. He exhibited in Paris.

Nameny, E., "Jewish Impressionists", in *Jewish Art, an illustrated history,* ed. by Cecil Roth, New York, 1971, pp. 207-228.

Abraham Mintchine (1898–1931)
B. in Kiev. In 1921 Mintchine began his career as a goldsmith's apprentice while studying painting and drawing. He left Russia in 1923 to go to Berlin where he remained until going to Paris in 1926. In Berlin he painted in a Cubist style and designed sets for the Hebrew Theatre. He participated in the Salon d'Automne, and the Salon des Indépendants while living in Paris. Mintchine's later works are characterized by intense and poetic use of color. He died during a visit to Provence.

George, W., "School of Paris", in *Jewish Art an illustrated history*, edited by Cecil Roth, New York, 1971, pp. 229–260.

Amedeo Modigliani (1884–1920)
B. in Leghorn, into a distinguished Italian-Jewish family. Before moving to Paris in 1906 Modigliani studied painting and sculpture in Florence and Venice. In Paris Modigliani—as a member of the Picasso-Max Jacob Circle—was sensitized to a lyrical yet sad expression of the human figure. His first contribution to the Salon des Indépendants in 1908, reflects his appreciation of varied sources—African sculpture, Cézanne, Picasso and Italian masters. He began sculpting in 1909 under the influence of his friend Brancusi. Usually referred to as a *peintre maudit*, Modigliani had his only major one-man show during his life time at the Berthe Weill Gallery, Paris (1917). Modigliani died in Paris and was subsequently honored at numerous retrospectives including the Venice Biennale (1930); The Museum of Modern Art, New York (1951); and the Boston Museum of Fine Arts, (1961).

Ceroni, A., *Amedeo Modigliani*, 2nd ed., Milan, 1965.

Mordecai Moreh (1937–   )
B. in Bagdad, Iraq. After emigrating to Israel in 1951, Moreh studied at the Bezalel School of Arts and Crafts, Jerusalem (1955–56). He continued his studies at the Accademia di Belle Arti, Florence (1960–62) and the Ecole des Beaux-Arts, Paris (1962) through scholarships from the Italian government and the America-Israel Culture Foundation, respectively. His precise graphics are mordant commentaries on the human condition. Influenced by Picasso's graphics, Moreh's work was first shown in Jerusalem in 1960. One-man exhibitions have been held at the Weyhe Gallery, New York (1966) and at the Gallery 10, Vienna (1969). Currently living in Paris, Moreh also participated in major print exhibitions at the British International Prints Biennale (1968, 1970).

New York Public Library, Prints Division, Artist File.

Jerome Myers (1867–1940)
B. in Petersburg, Virginia. Myers settled in New York in 1886 and worked as a scene painter for several theaters while pursuing his art studies at Cooper Union and the Art Students League, New York. His urban genre scenes were first exhibited in a one-man show at the Macbeth Gallery, New York (1908) and later in the Armory Show (1913). Like other members of the Robert Henri circle, Myers was also noted as a journalist and illustrator. He died in New York (1940) and that same year was honored by a memorial exhibition at the Whitney Museum of American Art, New York.

Myers, J., *Artist in Manhattan*, New York, 1940.

Abraham Naton (1909–1959)
B. in Bessarabia, Romania. From 1930 to 1933 he studied at the Bucharest Academy. He was active in the Zionist movement and moved to Palestine in 1935. Naton lived in Haifa, where he worked in the Lithography Institute. Between 1937 and 1938 he participated in exhibitions in Haifa and in 1940 he had a one-man show in Tel Aviv. Naton was a member of the New Horizons group, Tel Aviv, and frequently exhibited with them. He participated in the Biennale of Venice (1952) and the Biennale of São Paulo (1953).

The Tel Aviv Museum of Art, Artist File.

Louise Nevelson (1899–   )
B. in Kiev, Russia. Nevelson moved to Rockland, Maine in 1905. She studied at the Art Students League in New York and briefly in Germany with Hans Hofmann. Known primarily as a sculptor, she was included in *Young Sculptors* at the Brooklyn Museum (1935). Since then, she has had many one-woman shows in the United States and Europe and was represented at the Venice Biennale of 1962. Major retrospectives have been held at the Whitney Museum of American Art, New York (1966, 1970-71); the Rose Art Museum, Brandeis University, Waltham, Massachusetts (1967); the Rijksmuseum, Amsterdam (1969); and at the Walker Art Center, Minneapolis (1973). She lives in New York City.

Friedman, M., *Nevelson*, New York, 1973.

Barnett Newman (1905–1970)
B. in New York City. Newman received his BA from City College, New York (1927) and also studied at the Art Students League with Duncan Smith and John Sloan (1922–24) and (1929–30). Initially known to the art world as a polemicist, Newman organized the Writers-Artists ticket in 1933; regularly contributed to *Tiger's Eye* (1947–49), and with Baziotes, Motherwell, Hare, and Rothko co-founded The Subject of the Artist School, New York (1948). The least painterly of his generation of color field painters,

Newman, as a painter and sculptor, uses huge scale and monochromatic expanses to suggest his private metaphysics. His first one-man show was at Betty Parsons Gallery, New York (1950). Subsequent retrospectives have been held at Bennington College, Vermont (1958); The Solomon R. Guggenheim Museum, New York (1966); The Museum of Modern Art, New York (1971-2). D. in New York City.

Hess, T., *Barnett Newman*, New York, The Museum of Modern Art, 1971.

Abraham Ofek (1935-   )
B. in Bourgas, Bulgaria. In 1949, Ofek emigrated to Israel where he became a member of Kibbutz Ein-Hamifratz. He studied at the Accademia di Belle Arti, Florence (1958-60). Ofek painted a series of large murals at the Community Center, Kfar Uriah (1970). In 1972, he represented Israel at the Venice Biennale. Since his first one-man show at the Bezalel National Museum, Jerusalem (1957), he has had numerous exhibitions, notably at the Strozzi Palace, Florence (1959); The Tel Aviv Museum of Art (1972); and The Jewish Museum New York (1973). Ofek uses simplified forms, minimal details and earthy coloration in his bold compositions.

Kampf, A., *Ofek*, New York, The Jewish Museum, 1973.

Abel Pann (1883-1963)
B. in Kreslawka, Russia. The son of a rabbi who headed a yeshiva, Pann studied at the Vilna Academy (1895) and in Paris at the Académie Julien and with Bougereau and Toulouse-Lautrec. He travelled to Odessa, Vienna, and Palestine (1913-14). Until his return to Palestine in 1920 to teach again at the Bezalel School of Arts and Crafts, Jerusalem, Pann lived in Paris. Noted for his caricatures and paintings of the Russian pogroms, Pann also published illustrations for the Bible. D. in Jerusalem.

Thieme-Becker. *Kunstler—Lexikon*, Vol. XXVI, 1933-34, p. 286.

Harold Paris (1925-   )
B. in Edgemore, New York. With his father, a member of the Yiddish Art Theatre, Paris worked as a make-up man and actor (1941-43). In the US Army Corps of Engineers, and as *Stars and Stripes* Artist-Correspondent in the United States, England, France, and Germany (1943-46), Paris began to develop his strange and mystical vision. His multimedia constructions are intense evocations which render a private reading of humanity. He studied printmaking at the Atelier 17, New York (1949); at the Creative Lithographic workshop, New York (1951-52); and casting at the Munich Academy of Art on a Fulbright Fellowship for German studies (1955-56). The recipient of many awards including a

Guggenheim Grant (1953-54, 1954-55), Paris has had one-man shows since his first in 1951 at Argent Gallery, New York. These include: University Art Museum, Berkeley (1961); Hansen Gallery, San Francisco (1965, 1967); Studio Marconi, Milan (1969, 1972). Assistant Professor of art at the University of California, Berkeley, Paris shows at the Smith-Anderson Gallery in Palo Alto.

Selz, P. ed., *Harold Paris: The California Years*, Berkeley, 1972.

Jules Pascin (1885-1930)
B. Jules Pincas in Vidin, Bulgaria. Pascin studied in Munich (1903-04). First known as a cartoonist and illustrator for German periodicals, *Simplicissimus* and *Jugend*, Pascin moved to Paris in 1905 and was associated with the Montmartre and Montparnasse painters. In 1914 he emigrated to New York and became an American citizen (1920). An extensive traveler, Pascin's art ranges from local vignettes to erotic and satiric characterizations. Since his first one-man show at Paul Cassirer Gallery, Berlin (1910), he has had numerous international shows including the Galerie Bernheim-Jeune, Paris (1929); Bezalel National Museum, Jerusalem (1958); and University Art Museum, Berkeley (1966). Pascin died by suicide in Paris.

Warnod, A., *Pascin*, Monte Carlo, 1954.

Leonid Pasternak (1862-1945)
B. in Odessa. Pasternak studied medicine in Moscow but in 1883 went to the Munich Art Academy. In 1884 he was appointed Professor of art at the Moscow Academy of Fine Arts, where he taught for twenty-five years. Pasternak founded the "Russian Artists Union" and frequently exhibited portraits there. During the 1917 Russian Revolution he went to Berlin. He visited Palestine in 1924, where he painted portraits of distinguished personalities. During World War II he went to England, where he died. Today, Pasternak, a celebrated portrait painter of his time, is best known as the father of Boris Pasternak, the novelist.

Osborn, M., *Leonid Pasternak*, Warsaw, 1932.

Antoine Pevsner (1886-1962)
B. in Orel, Russia. Pevsner studied at the School of Fine Arts, Kiev (1902-09); the St. Petersburg Academy (1910), and then in Paris (1912, 1913-14). In Paris he was introduced to Cubism by his friends Archipenko and Modigliani and was greatly impressed by the Eiffel Tower. Pevsner returned to Russia (1914) before joining his brother Naum Gabo in Oslo (1915-16), where he turned from abstract painting to sculpture. When Pevsner returned to Russia in 1917, he

taught at the Moscow Academy of Fine Arts, with Kandinsky and Malevich. In 1920 he and Gabo conceived the *Realist Manifesto* in which they argued that void (not mass), is the fundamental of sculpture. Pevsner left Russia in 1923 and settled permanently in Paris. He became a French citizen in 1930 and received The French Legion of Honor (1961). In Paris he joined the *Abstraction-Création* group with Gabo, Herbin, Kupka, and Mondrian (1931), and co-founding *Réalités-Nouvelles* (1946). Pevsner and Gabo have been given a joint retrospective at The Museum of Modern Art, New York (1966). Pevsner had a retrospective at Musée National d' Art Moderne, Paris (1957), and a special room for his work at the Venice Biennale XXIX (1959). D. in Paris.

Peissi, P. and Giedion-Welcker, C., *Antoine Pevsner*, Neuchâtel, 1961.

Nathan Rapoport (1911-   )
B. in Warsaw, Poland. Rapoport studied art at the Academy of Art, Warsaw; the Ecole des Beaux-Arts, Paris; and informally in Italy and France. The recipient of numerous awards since his youth in Poland, Rapoport achieved notoriety for refusing to allow his sculpture *Tennis* to enter the Olympics Exhibition in Berlin (1936). A major preoccupation of his heroic figurative sculpture is memorialization of the victims of the Holocaust. His monumental commissions include: Ghetto Monument, on the site of the Warsaw Ghetto; and Mordechai Anilewicz Memorial at Yad Vashem in Israel; the Monument for the Jewish Heroes of World War II in Paris; and *Last March* in Dallas, Texas. Rapoport resides in New York and Israel and frequently participates in Jewish events.

Glass, A., "Never to Forget", *The Jewish Standard*, May 15, 1972, pp. 1-4.

Abraham Rattner (1895-   )
B. in Poughkeepsie, New York. From 1913 to 1914, Rattner studied at George Washington University and the Corcoran School of Art in Washington, D. C. After World War I, he resumed his education at the Ecole des Beaux-Arts in Paris, settling there until 1940. Forced to flee Paris, he returned to the United States and toured the country with Henry Miller. Since his first one-man show at the Galerie Bonjean, Paris (1935) he has had numerous exhibitions—Paul Rosenberg and Company, New York (1943, 1944, 1946, 1948, 1950, 1956), Art Institute of Chicago (1955), A.F.A. Gallery, New York (1959-60). Rattner designed a stained glass window wall for New Synagogue, Chicago (1960). His work, inspired both by Old Testament themes and contemporary Jewish history, combines aspects of French and German Expressionism. Rattner lives in New York City.

Leepa, A., *Abraham Rattner*, New York, forthcoming 1976-77.

Bernard Reder (1897-1963)
B. in Bukovina, Austria. At the Academy of Fine Arts, Prague in 1919 Reder studied graphic art with Peter Bromse and sculpture with Jan Stursa. Returning to Bukovina in 1922 Reder worked as a stonemason. Not until 1930, two years after his first one-man exhibition of watercolors in Prague, did Reder devote his entire efforts to sculpture. His woodcuts and sculpture, rich in fantasy, embroider his Hasidic background into baroque conceptions based on realistic forms. Since his first one-man exhibition of sculpture in 1935 at the Manes Gallery, Prague, Reder has become internationally known through exhibitions at Wildenstein Gallery, Paris (1940); World House Gallery, New York, at the Whitney Museum of American Art, New York (1961); and at The Tel Aviv Museum of Art (1968). Reder lived and worked in New York from 1958 until his death.

Baur, J., *Bernard Reder*, New York, 1961.

Olly Ritterband (1923-   )
B. in Transylvania, Romania. In 1944 Ritterband was transported to Auschwitz, in 1945 to Bergen-Belsen, and later to Sweden. Interested in mosaic art work since 1950, Ritterband learned the technique at the Ecole des Beaux-Arts, Paris. In both her paintings and mosaics, she effects the horrors of the concentration camps in a manner that recalls Edvard Munch. Since her first one-woman exhibition at the National Museum of Denmark (1971), Ritterband has participated in numerous group exhibitions—the Rostock Museum, Germany (1973) and The Tel Aviv Museum of Art (1975). Ritterband lives in Copenhagen.

Correspondence with artist.

Larry Rivers (1923-   )
B. in the Bronx, New York. Larry Rivers first studied at the Julliard School of Music, New York (1944) and then played the jazz saxophone in New York. He studied painting at the Hans Hofmann School of Art (1947-48) and at New York University (1948-50). Noted for his critical interpretation of both art historical and popular commercial images, Rivers' work balances readable references against a lively gestural technique. Rivers, a transitional figure between Abstract Expressionism and Pop Art, has played an active part in the non-establishment New York literary and painting scene since his first one-man show at New York's Jane Street Gallery (1949). Major one-man exhibitions have been held at The Jewish Museum, New York (1965); the Art Institute of Chicago (1970), and Rice University, Houston (1971). Rivers lives in New York City.

Hunter, S., *Larry Rivers*, New York, 1970.

Mark Rothko (1903–1970)
B. in Dvinsk, Russia. Rothko's family emigrated to Portland, Oregon in 1913. He studied at Yale University (1921–23), and at the Art Students League, New York with Max Weber in 1925. His formative years include such activities as co-founding The Ten with Ilya Bolotowsky and Adolph Gottlieb (1935); working on the WPA Federal Arts Project, New York (1936–37); and co-founding The Subject of the Artists School, New York (1948). A color field painter within the tradition of Romanticism, Rothko reached his general format—color rectangles floating on a color ground—by 1950. A group of abstract, evocative works has been permanently installed in the Rothko Room at the Tate Gallery, London since 1970. This more heroic vein was also realized in murals for Harvard University and in the Rothko Chapel at St. Thomas University, Houston, Texas. Rothko has been honored by retrospectives at The Museum of Modern Art, New York (1961); at The Solomon R. Guggenheim Museum, New York (1963), and at the Kunsthaus Zurich (1971–72). Rothko died by suicide in New York.

Selz, P., *Mark Rothko*, New York, The Museum of Modern Art, 1961.

Reuven Rubin (1893–1975)
B. in Gabatz, Romania. Rubin was brought up in a traditional Jewish home. He studied at The Bezalel School of Arts and Crafts, Jerusalem (1912), in Paris at the Ecole des Beaux-Arts and the Académie Collarossi (1913–14), and in Italy. His reputation as a painter/sculptor of Jewish folk themes was established during his stay in Romania (1916–19). Since his first one-man show, sponsored by Alfred Stieglitz at the Anderson Gallery, New York (1920); he has had numerous international exhibitions, which include the inaugural show at The Tel Aviv Museum of Art (1932); in Tel Aviv in 1947 and 1955; and at Wildenstein and Company, New York (1962). Until World War II Rubin designed scenery and costumes for the Habimah and other Israeli theatre companies. Noted for his commitment to art in Israel, Rubin helped to create and chaired The Association of Painters and Sculptors of Palestine (1912–37). His honors include a prize from the city of Tel Aviv for artistic achievement (1964). Rubin died in Caesarea.

Wilkinson, S., *Reuven Rubin*, New York, [1974].

Issachar Ryback (1897–1935)
B. in Elisabethgrad, Russia. Ryback studied art in Kiev and in 1917 was appointed drawing teacher by the Jewish Cultural League. Ryback associated with the Constructivists while in Moscow (1919–21) and the Russian Jewish artists living in Paris (1926). His paintings and ceramic works depict characters drawn from Jewish folklore and ghetto life. Ryback exhibited in Berlin (1924) and at Wildenstein and Company, Paris (1935). A permanent installation of his work is on view at Ryback House, Ramat Yosef, Israel.

Cogniat, R., *Ryback*, Paris, 1935.

Shalom Seba (1897–   )
B. in Tilsit, Russia. Seba studied painting and architecture at the Berlin Academy of Art. He travelled in the Far East in 1926. In 1933 Seba left Germany and went to Switzerland and Sweden, where he worked in film. In 1936 he went to Israel, lived in Givat'aim, designed sets for the Habima Theatre, and executed murals and stained glass windows. He has had one-man exhibitions at The Tel Aviv Museum of Art (1945, 1955, 1961). Seba moved to Germany in the early 1960s.

The Tel Aviv Museum of Art, Artist File.

Lazar Segall (1891–1957)
B. in Vilna, Lithuania. Emigrating to Berlin in 1906, Segall studied at the Academy of Fine Arts in Berlin (1907–09). Since his first one-man exhibition at the Gurlitt Gallery, Dresden (1910), Segall worked within a German Expressionist style. In his paintings, engravings and sculpture, which have been internationally exhibited since 1926, Segall expresses human tragedy as experienced in contemporary history. He has had retrospective exhibitions at the Venice Biennale (1958) and Musée d'Art Moderne, Paris (1959). In 1923, Segall emigrated to Brazil where he lived until his death.

Bardi, P.M., *Lazar Segall*, São Paulo, 1959.

Kurt Seligmann (1900–1961)
B. in Basel, Switzerland. After studying at the Geneva Academy of Art, Seligmann lived in Paris (1929–39). A member of the Surrealist and *Abstraction-Création* groups, his magical paintings and illustrations reflect his metamorphic, imaginative visions of man and nature. Since his first one-man show at Galerie Bucher, Paris (1932), Seligmann has had numerous exhibitions—Ruth White Gallery, New York (1960), D'Arcy Galleries, New York (1964). A versatile talent, Seligmann is an authority on witchcraft. The author of *The Mirror of Magic* (1946), costume designer for a ballet by Balanchine (1947), Seligmann died in Sugar Loaf, New York where he had lived since 1939.

Myers, B., "Puppets of Kurt Seligmann—an Homage", *Craft Horizon*, December 1970, pp. 33–5.

Ben Shahn (1898–1969)
B. in Kovno, Lithuania. Shahn's parents
emigrated to New York. Apprenticed to a
lithographer (1911–17), Shahn worked
intermittently as a lithographer until 1930. His
art education included classes at the National
Academy of Design, the Art Students League,
and the Educational Alliance Art School, all in
New York, as well as European travel and study.
From 1931 to 1933, he was a mural assistant to
Diego Rivera and worked on the RCA Building at
Rockefeller Center in New York. A versatile
talent, Shahn has illustrated books, notably the
Alphabet of Creation and designed sets for Jerome
Robbins' ballets. His socially conscious
illustrations, graphics and paintings have been
honored by retrospectives at The Museum of
Modern Art, New York (1961), and the New
Jersey State Museum, Trenton (1969). Shahn
lived in Hightstown, New Jersey.

Shahn, B., *Ben Shahn*, New York, 1972.

Johanon Simon (1905–   )
B. in Berlin. Simon studied at the Berlin Art
Academy (1924), the Bauhaus (1925), Munich Art
Academy (1926) and in Frankfurt with Max
Beckmann. Living in Paris (1928–36), he joined
the circle of painters around Derain. He travelled
to New York (1935), before settling permanently
in Palestine (1936). Since his first one–man show
at Castel Gallery, Paris (1935), he has participated
in numerous exhibitions as a member of Kibbutz
Gan–Shmuel, and of The Painters and Sculptors
Association of Israel. Influenced by Diego Rivera
and travel in Latin America (1954), Simon is
noted for his wall paintings in kibbutzim,
factories and public institutions in Israel.
Currently living near Herzelia, Simon also
maintains a studio in Ein Hod, Israel.

Correspondence with artist.

Mitchell Siporin (1910–   )
B. in New York City. Siporin studied at the Art
Institute of Chicago School. A participant in the
WPA Federal Arts Project, Mural Division,
Siporin received commissions for Post Offices in
Decatur, Illinois (1935) and in St. Louis, Missouri
(1939). He exhibited regularly at The Downtown
Gallery, New York from 1940. He participated in
group shows at The Museum of Modern Art,
New York (1939, 1942). Siporin, Professor of
painting at Brandeis University, Waltham,
Massachusetts since 1951, works in an
Expressionist style, and favors figurative
landscape themes.

Whitney Museum of American Art, New York,
Artist File.

Chaim Soutine (1893–1943)
B. in Smilovitchi, near Minsk, Lithuania. With
Michael Kiköine, Soutine attended the Vilna

Academy of Fine Arts (1910–13). Soutine
continued his studies in 1913 at the Ecole des
Beaux–Arts and at the Atelier Cormon. There he
met Chagall, Laurens, Lipchitz, and Modigliani.
A *peintre maudit,* Soutine developed his tragic
vision in an Expressionist idiom. In Céret
(1919–22), his feverish compositions—landscapes,
still lifes, portraits—increasingly reflect his
preoccupation with wild, sumptuous color.
Soutine lived in Paris (1925–39); he went into
hiding until 1943. Since his first one–man
exhibition at the Galerie Bing, Paris (1927)
Soutine has been honored by exhibitions at the
Galerie de France, Paris (1945); The Museum of
Modern Art, New York (1950) and the Los
Angeles County Museum of Art (1968). D. in
Paris.

Tuchman, M., *Chaim Soutine*, Los Angeles, Los
Angeles County Museum of Art, 1968.

Issac Soyer (1902–   )
B. in Tombov, Russia. Soyer moved with his
family to America in 1913. Like his older twin
brothers, Moses and Raphael, he studied in New
York at the National Academy of Design, Cooper
Union, the Educational Alliance Art School, and
in Paris and Madrid. Committed to teaching as
well as painting he has taught in New York at the
Educational Alliance, and the New School for
Social Research. Soyer has had one–man
exhibitions at the Midtown Gallery, New York
(1936); and at the Albright Art Gallery, Buffalo
(1942). His works realize the drama of ordinary
city life and people. Soyer lives in New York.

Soyer, M., "Three Brothers", *Magazine of Art,*
April 1939, pp. 201–207, 254.

Moses Soyer (1899–1974)
B. in Borisoglebsk, Russia. Soyer emigrated to
New York in 1913 and became a United States
citizen in 1925. Like his twin brother, Raphael,
Moses' early studies in New York were at
Cooper Union, the National Academy of Design,
and the Educational Alliance Art School. He
participated in the WPA Federal Arts Project,
and taught at the New School for Social
Research, New York for many years. Soyer's
mature work continued to depict urban-social
scenes. Moses Soyer's works were exhibited
regularly from 1944 at the ACA Gallery, New
York and a retrospective was held at Syracuse
University, New York (1972). D. in New York.

Willard, C., *Moses Soyer*, New York, 1962.

Raphael Soyer (1899–   )
B. in Borisoglebsk, Russia, twin of Moses Soyer.
Soyer and his family emigrated to New York in
1913. He studied and later taught at the Art
Students League of New York. Known primarily
as an urban-realist painter, Soyer's memoir, *Self
Revealment* (1962), similarly shows his human-

itarian values. His work has been included in the Whitney Museum of American Art, *Annual* (1934–72). In 1953 he co-founded *Reality* magazine. He has had many one-man shows in New York and was honored with a retrospective at the Whitney Museum of American Art, New York (1967). He lives in New York.

Goodrich, L., *Raphael Soyer*, New York, 1972.

Jacob Steinhardt (1881–1968)
B. in Zerkow, Russia. Steinhardt studied at the Museum of Arts and Crafts in Berlin (1906), with Louis Corinth and Herman Struck. In 1909, he moved to Paris where he worked with Laurens, Steinlen, and Matisse. He returned to Germany and together with Ludwig Meidner and Richard Janthus founded the *Pathetiker* group in 1912. Settling in Jerusalem (1933), he was the Head of the Graphic Department of the Bezalel School of Arts and Crafts and its Director (1953–57). Steinhardt has participated in numerous group exhibitions; Der Sturm Gallery, Berlin (1912); Berlin Secession (1917); and had one-man exhibitions at Gurlitt Gallery, Munich (1958); Palace of the Legion of Honor, San Francisco (1959); and the Walthen-Rathenau Saal, Berlin (1973). Awards for his graphics, frequently of social and religious themes, include the first international prize in graphic arts, at the São Paulo Biennale (1955) and the Liturgica Prize at the Venice Biennale (1960). D. in Jerusalem.

Pfefferkorn, R., *Jacob Steinhardt*, Berlin, 1973.

Herman Struck (1876–1944)
B. in Berlin. Struck studied etching at the Berlin Academy with Max Kone. Committed to Zionist and Orthodox Judaism throughout his life, Struck, during one of his several study trips throughout Europe, visited Palestine in 1903. Before moving to Palestine in 1923, Struck was known in Germany as a master craftsman, teacher, illustrator and author of a popular book on graphics, *The Art of Etching*. He taught Chagall, Liebermann, Israels, and Corinth and was one of the few German members of the London Royal Society of Painters, Etchers, and Engravers. His characteristic depiction of scenes from Jewish life, portraits and urban landscapes, have been shown in numerous international exhibitions— Berlin Photograph Gallery, New York (1913) the Seligman Gallery, New York (1928). D. in Haifa.

Donath, A., *Herman Struck*, Berlin, 1920.

Anna Ticho (1894–   )
B. in Brno, Moravia. Ticho spent her childhood in Vienna where she studied painting and drawing. Emigrating to Palestine in 1912, she settled in Jerusalem. Ticho has had one-woman shows notably at Bezalel National Museum, Jerusalem (1959); the Art Institute of Chicago (1964); and The Jewish Museum, New York

(1969). Ticho lives in Jerusalem—and the interpretation of its landscape is the major subject of her drawings.

Cohen, E., *The Drawings of Anna Ticho*, New York, The Jewish Museum, 1969.

Jennings Tofel (1891–1959)
B. in Poland. Tofel emigrated to America in 1905 and lived in New York City throughout his life. An Expressionist writer and painter, Tofel began his career within the Stieglitz circle. His first one-man show at Bourgeois Galleries, New York (1919) was followed by shows at Artist Gallery, New York (1947, 1952, 1954, 1956, 1958) and at Zabriskie Gallery, New York (1964). Tofel, who frequently painted Old Testament themes, wrote a monograph on the artist Benjamin Kopman. Tofel died in New York City.

New York Public Library, Art Division, Artist File.

Igael Tumarkin (1933–   )
B. in Dresden. Taken to Palestine in 1935, Tumarkin lived and studied in Germany, Holland and Paris (1955–61). In Berlin, he worked as a stage designer for the Berlin Ensemble. His painting and sculpture is characterized by subjective symbolism. Since his first one-man exhibition at the Galerie Sante Landiver, Berlin (1956), Tumarkin has had numerous exhibitions—The Israel Museum, Jerusalem (1964); Byron Gallery, New York (1970); The Tel Aviv Museum of Art (1974); The Jewish Museum, New York (1974). Currently living in New York, Tumarkin continues to voice his painful vision of man in relation to his environment in his art.

Tumarkin, I., *Tumarkin by Tumarkin: 1957–1970*, Tel Aviv, 1970.

Abraham Walkowitz (1878–1965)
B. in Tyumen, Russia. Walkowitz emigrated to New York in 1886 where he studied at Cooper Union and later taught at the Educational Alliance Art School, both in New York. Living in Paris (1906–09), his paintings and drawings reflect a synthesis of contemporary avant-garde trends—Fauvism and Cubism. His broad range of subject matter, from the well known Isadora Duncan drawings, to scenes of the Lower East Side gained reputation through various exhibitions including a major retrospective at The Jewish Museum, New York (1949). D. in New York.

Hunter, S., *American Art of the 20th Century*, New York, 1972.

Max Weber (1881–1961)
B. in Bialystok, Russia. Weber emigrated to New York in 1891. Before moving to Paris to study with Henri Matisse, he had studied art at the

Pratt Institute, New York. Returning to New York in 1909, Weber taught at the Art Students League through the 1920s. A member of the Steiglitz circle, Weber was noted for his personal synthesis of avant-garde European trends—Fauvism, Cubism and Expressionismn. His major retrospectives include The Museum of Modern Art, New York (1930); the Whitney Museum of American Art, New York (1949); The Jewish Museum, New York (1956). D. in Great Neck, New York.

Werner, A., *Max Weber*, New York, 1975.

Elbert Weinberg (1928-   )
B. in Hartford, Connecticut. Weinberg earned a certificate from the Hartford Art School (1948), a BFA from Rhode Island School of Design (1951), an MFA from Yale University (1955). Awarded a Guggenheim Grant (1960), Weinberg has participated in frequent group exhibitions—*Sculpture, U.S.A.*, The Museum of Modern Art, New York (1959); and the Whitney Museum of American Art, *Annual*, New York (1954, 1958, 1960, 1964, 1965). Weinberg's paintings and sculpture often contain Biblical, specifically Jewish, content. He lives in Rome, New York.

Borgenicht Gallery, New York, Artist Biography.

Hendrik Werkman (1882-1945)
B. in Groningen, the Netherlands. Werkman worked as a journalist and as an amateur photographer while learning printmaking. By 1912 he founded his own print shop and in 1923 published *The Next Call*, an avant-garde print journal. First exhibiting with the *Circle et Carré* group (1930), Werkman had his first one-man exhibition at Spoor Gallery, Amsterdam (1939). Until his arrest by the Nazis in 1945, Werkman continued to experiment with printmaking in a manner derived from the Futurist, Dada, and Bauhaus artists. His abstract and figurative prints were known as illustrations for the *Blaue Schuit* and M. Buber's *Die Legende des Baalschem.* Werkman was executed by the Nazis in 1945.

Muller, F., ed., *H. N. Werkman*, Teufen, 1964.

Joseph Zaritsky (1891-   )
B. in Borislav, Russia. Zaritsky graduated from the Kiev Art Academy (1914) and emigrated to Palestine in 1923. Before settling permanently in Tel Aviv, he studied in Paris (1927-29). One of the founders of the New Horizon Group, Tel Aviv (1948), Zaritsky participated in the Venice Biennale (1948). Zaritsky's watercolors and draw-ings—primarily landscapes—are characterized by their lyricism. He had a one-man show at the Stedelijk Museum, Amsterdam (1955) and participated in *Art Israel*, The Museum of

Modern Art, New York (1964). The recipient of the Israel Prize for Art (1960), Zaritsky lives in Tel Aviv.

Seitz, W., *Art Israel*, New York, The Museum of Modern Art, 1964.

William Zorach (1887-1966)
B. in Eurburg, Lithuania. Zorach emigrated with his family to Ohio in 1891. He studied at Cleveland Museum School of Art from 1902 to 1905; in New York at the Art Students League, and the National Academy of Design (1907-10) and in Paris at La Palette (1910-11). Earning a living as a commercial lithographer, Zorach had his first one-man show at the Taylor Gallery, Cleveland (1912). Until 1917 Zorach painted in a manner typical of his generation of American artists, reflecting his assimilation of Fauvist and Cubist innovations. He abandoned painting in 1917 to explore the figurative tradition in sculpture. Zorach, essentially an academic sculptor, creates works that evoke feelings of emotion and strength. Retrospectives of his work have been held at the Whitney Museum of American Art, New York (1959), and the Danenberg Gallery, New York (1970). Zorach was married to Marguerite Zorach, the sculptor. D. in Bath, Maine.

Baur, J., *William Zorach*, New York, 1959.

Jacques Zucker (1900-   )
B. in Radom, Poland. Running away from home in 1913, Zucker fled to Palestine where he studied at The Bezalel School of Arts and Crafts, Jerusalem. His art studies continued in Paris at the Julien and Calarossi Académies after World War I. A member of the School of Paris, Zucker paints landscapes, still lifes, and interiors characterized by their color, immediacy, and evocation of inner serenity. Since his first one-man show in 1927 at the Raleigh Gallery, New York, Zucker has had international exhibitions—at The Tel Aviv Museum of Art (1950), and the Galerie Pétridès, Paris (1960), and he exhibits at Schoneman Galleries, New York. He lives in New York.

Roger-Marx, C., *Jacques Zucker*, Paris, 1971.

Compiled by Peninah Petruck.

Selected Bibliography

Beresniak, D. *Aspects de l'art juif.* Paris: Temps Present, 1960.

Cohn-Wiener, E. *Die Jüdische Kunst.* Berlin, 1929.

Cusin, S. *Art in the Jewish Tradition.* Milan: Adei-Wizo, 1963.

Eichenbaum, P. *Memorial Exhibition: Jewish Artists Who Perished In The Holocaust.* Tel Aviv: The Tel Aviv Museum of Art, 1968.

Fischer, Y., Roth, C., and Werner, A. "Art." *Encyclopedia Judaica,* Jerusalem: Keter Publishing Ltd., 1971, pp. 499-594.

Fischer, Y. *Expressionism in Eretz-Israel in the Thirties And Its Ties with the Ecole de Paris.* Jerusalem: The Israel Museum, 1971.

Gamzu, A. *Painting and Sculpture in Israel.* Tel Aviv: Eschcol Publishers, 1951.

————. *Sculpture in Israel.* Tel Aviv: Eschcol Publishers, 1957.

Gordis, R. and Davidowitz, M., eds. *Art in Judaism.* N.Y.: National Council on Art in Jewish Life, 1975.

Gutfeld, L. *Jewish Art from the Bible to Chagall.* N.Y.: T. Yoseloff, 1968.

Gutman, J. "Jewish Art: The Modern Era." *Encyclopedia of Art,* 1963, VIII, pp. 920-21.

Herman, J. "On Being a Jewish Artist." *Jewish Quarterly,* Autumn, 1964.

The Jewish Museum. *Inaugural Exhibition.* N.Y.: The Jewish Museum, 1949.

Kampf, A. "The Jewish Museum—An Institution Adrift." *Judaism,* Summer, 1968.

Katz, K. "Painting and Sculpture in Israel." *Atlantic Monthly,* November, 1961, pp. 100–110.

Landsberger, F. *History of Jewish Art.* Cinncinati: Union of Hebrew Congregations, 1946.

Lozowick, L. *100 Contemporary American Jewish Painters and Sculptors.* N.Y.: Yiddisher Kultur Farband, 1949.

Mayer, L. *Bibliography of Jewish Art.* Jerusalem: Magnes Press, 1967.

Naimenyi, E. *The Essence of Jewish Art.* N.Y., 1960.

Rabinowitz, J. "Jewish Personalities in Modern American Painting." *Reflex,* Nov., 1935, pp. 26-8.

Rosenberg, H. "Is there Jewish Art?" *Commentary,* July, 1966.

Rosenberg, J. ed. *Bezalel: Its Aim and Purpose.* Jerusalem: American Friends of Bezalel, 1935.

Rosenau, H. *A Short History of Jewish Art.* London: J. Clarke, 1948.

Roth, C. ed. *Jewish Art, an illustrated history.* N.Y.: McGraw Hill, 1971.

Rubens, A. *A Jewish Iconography.* London, 1954.

Schwarz, K. *Jewish Artists in the 19th and 20th Centuries.* N.Y.: Philosophical Library, 1949.

————. *Jewish Sculptors.* Jerusalem: Art Publishers, 1954.

Seitz, W. *Art Israel: 26 Painters and Sculptors.* N.Y.: The Museum of Modern Art, 1964.

Shatz, B. *Bezalel Exhibition: Palestine Arts and Crafts.* Jerusalem: Bezalel School of Arts, 1926, 2nd ed. 1939.

Shechori, R. *Art in Israel.* Tel Aviv: Sudan Publishing House, 1974.

Strauss, H. *Die Kunst der Juden in Wandel der Zeit und Umwelt—Das Juden problem in Spiegel der Kunst.* Tübingen: Verlag Ernst Wasmuth, 1972.

Talphir, G. *Israel Painters.* Tel Aviv: Gazith Art Publishing, 1953.

————. *Modern Jewish Painters.* Tel Aviv: Gazith Art Publishing, 1938.

Trends in Israeli Art. Jerusalem: The Israel Museum, 1965.

Wigoder, G. ed. *Jewish Art and Civilization.* N.Y.: Walker Publishing Co., 1972.

Zucker, J. "On the Present State of art, with a word to certain Jewish painters," *Menorah Journal,* (34:1) pp. 104–8.

Photographic Credits

Victor Amato, Washington, D.C.
The Art Institute of Chicago
J. J. Breit, New York
Geoffrey Clements, New York
Department of Art, Brown University, Providence
Ran Erde, Tel Aviv
eeva-inkeri, New York
John R. Freeman, London
Bruce C. Jones, New York
Peter J. Juley and Son, New York
Kennedy Galleries, Inc., New York
Leeds City Art Galleries, England
Mishkan Le'Omanut, Ein Harod
Museum of Art, University of Iowa, Des Moines
The Museum of Modern Art, New York
Gail Nathan, New York
Eric Pollitzer, New York
Nathan Rabin, New York
Zev Radovan, Jerusalem
Städelsches Kunstinstitut und Städtische Galerie, Frankfurt
Armand Tornow, São Paulo
Whitney Museum of American Art, New York
I. Zafrir, Tel Aviv

Index to Artists in the Exhibition

Chronology of Events

Date	History	Culture	Publications
1870			Leopold Löw publishes *Graphische Requisiten und Erzeugnisse bei den Juden*, Leipzig
1872			Vladimir Stasov, art historian, publishes "On the Occasion of the Construction of the Synagogue of St. Petersburg", and "A Jewish Generation in the Creation of a European Art", in *Evreiskaia Biblioteka: istoriko-literaturnyi sbornik* [periodical]
1875		Founding of Art Students League, NYC	
1876		Abraham Goldfaden establishes Yiddish Theater in Jassi, Romania	Heinrich Graetz completes *Geschichte der Juden (History of the Jews)*
			George Eliot completes *Daniel Deronda*
1878		Exhibition of Jewish ceremonial art from the collection of Joseph Strauss at the Universal Exhibition at the Trocadero, Paris	
1881	Wave of pogroms in Southern Russia followed by mass emigration which brought over two million Jews to the U.S.; 350,000 to Western Europe; 60,000 to Palestine (to 1914)		Laurence Oliphant publishes *Land of Gilead*
	Am Olam (Eternal People) Organization founded in Odessa to settle Jews in American communes		
1882	Am Olam establishes "New Odessa", Jewish socialist commune near Portland, Oregon	First Yiddish play, *Machashefa (The Witch)*, performed in NYC, by The Hebrew Opera and Dramatic Company	Leon Pinsker publishes *Autoemanzipation*
	Bilu, 1st organized group of pioneers, established in Russia, settles in Palestine		Emma Lazarus writes *Epistle to the Hebrews*

Date	History	Culture	Publications
1883		L. Pasternak goes to Munich and enrolls in Academy of Art	
1886		A. Walkowitz, age 8, moves with family from Russia to U.S.	
1887		The Jewish Theological Seminary of America established in NYC	
1888	The United Hebrew Trades (Vereinigte Yiddishe Gevergschaften) founded; parent institution of the Jewish Labor Movement		Jewish Publication Society of America established
1889		Educational Alliance Art School founded in NYC, on the Lower East Side	Founding of *The Jewish Quarterly Review*, England
1890		Art Nouveau spreads throughout European centers (1890-1900)	
1891	Expulsion of Jews from Moscow	Bernard Berenson, art historian, converts to Catholicism M. Weber, age 10, arrives in U.S. with family, from Bialystock, Russia W. Zorach, age 4, emigrates to U.S. from Lithuania with family	
1892		Yehuda Pen opens art school in Vitebsk	Israel Zangwill publishes *Children of the Ghetto*, London
1893		Hadji Ephraim Benguiat Collection of Jewish ceremonial objects exhibited at the World's Columbian Exposition, Chicago	
1894	Start of Dreyfus affair in France	E.M. Lilien arrives in Munich from Cracow	Discovery of *Sarajevo Haggada*, 14th century illuminated manuscript; published with commentary by Mueller and Schlosser, with first survey of Hebrew illuminated manuscript by David Kaufmann
1896		Artist Mark Gertler emigrates with family from Przemysl, Galicia to London	Discovery of Cairo Genizah, storehouse of literary and historical documents Theodor Herzl publishes *Der Judenstaat (The Jewish State)*, Vienna
1897	Bund founded (General Jewish Workers Union in Lithuania, Poland and Russia) First Zionist Congress, Basle	Establishment of Jewish Museum, Vienna	
1900		J. Kramer, age 8, emigrates with family from Ukraine to Leeds, England	Sigmund Freud publishes *Die Traumdeutung (The Interpretation of Dreams)*, Germany

Date	History	Culture	Publications
1900 cont.			*Jewish Daily Forward* begins publication in New York under editorship of Abraham Cahan *Ost und West*, an illustrated monthly for modern Jewry with contributions by artists, scholars and writers, Berlin
1901	Founding of Poalei Zion, Socialist Zionist organization, active in Russia, Europe, Palestine, and U.S.	The Jewish Museum, and the Society for Exploration of Jewish Antiquities, established in Frankfurt	
1903	With pogrom in Kishinev, new wave of pogroms in Russia begins	Moshe Oved arrives in London from Poland and founds Cameo Corner, a shop for antique jewelry	Vladimir Stasov and David Guenzburg publish *L'ornement hébreu*
1904	Russo–Japanese War (1904–1905)		
1905	Abortive Revolution in Russia	Edward Steichen and Alfred Stieglitz jointly found New York's Little Gallery of the Photo–Secession, later known as 291 Gallery Warburg Bibliothek founded in Hamburg by Aby Warburg Expressionist Group *Die Brücke* established in Berlin Fauve movement in Paris J. Pascin goes from Munich to Paris J. Epstein leaves U.S. and settles in London M. Weber leaves U.S. for Paris A. Modigliani settles in Paris L. Nevelson, age 6, and her family emigrate from Kiev to U.S. E. M. Lilien moves from Berlin to Jerusalem J. Tofel moves from Poland to U.S.	Albert Einstein publishes essay, "The Spatial Theory of Relativity"
1906	Peak of immigration to U.S.; 642,000 Jews arrive (1906–1909)	Founding of the Jewish Museum, Prague The Bezalel School of Arts and Crafts founded in Jerusalem under direction of sculptor Boris Shatz B. Shahn emigrates with family from Kovno to U.S. A. Walkowitz leaves NYC for Paris	Martin Buber publishes *Die Geschichten das Rabbi Nachman* Hayim Joseph Brenner, Yiddish and Hebrew writer, publishes *Ha-Meorer (The Awakener)* [periodical], London

Date	History	Culture	Publications
1906 cont.		L. Lozowick, age 14, emigrates to U.S. from Kiev	
		Picasso paints *Les Demoiselles d'Avignon* (1906–07); start of Cubism	
1907		Writer Shmuel Agnon goes to Palestine	Heinrich Kohl and Carl Watzinger publish results of their excavation of ancient Galilean synagogues which uncovered sculpted friezes
		S. Hirszenberg joins faculty at Bezalel School of Arts and Crafts	
		Artists Georges Kars and Louis Marcoussis go to Paris	
		Meyer Schapiro, art historian, brought by his family from Lithuania to U.S.	
1908		Establishment of Jewish Historical and Ethnological Society in St. Petersburg headed by S. An-Ski	
		Exhibition of Ashcan School paintings by The Eight, at Macbeth Gallery, NYC	
1909	First collective workers' settlement (kibbutz) founded in Palestine	Leon Bakst, theatre designer, arrives in Paris	Louis Ginzberg publishes *The Legends of the Jews*, a collection from the Talmudic literature
	Founding of Tel Aviv	J. Lipchitz, age 18, arrives in Paris from Lithuania	*Evreiskaia starina (Jewish Antiquity)* journal published in St. Petersburg (1909-16)
1910		Establishment of Jewish Museum in Warsaw	
		First issue of *Der Sturm* published in Berlin by Herwarth Walden	
		M. Chagall arrives in Paris from Vitebsk, via St. Petersburg	
		Moise Kisling arrives in Paris	
1911		M. Kantor moves to U.S. from Russia	
		Expressionist group *Blaue Reiter* in Munich	
		An-Ski leads Jewish ethnographic expedition through the villages of Volhynia and Podolia	
1912		David Bomberg, Jacob Kramer, Mark Gertler, and Isaac Rosenfeld students at the Slade School of Art, London	

Date	History	Culture	Publications
1912 cont.		A. Pevsner arrives in Paris from Russia	
		R. Rubin goes from Romania to Jerusalem to study at Bezalel School of Arts and Crafts	
		A. Ticho arrives in Jerusalem from Vienna	
		Three brothers, Moses, Raphael and Isaac Soyer, arrive with their family in U.S. from Russia	
		M. Chagall paints *Calvary* in Paris	
		Benno Schotz goes from Lithuania to Glasgow, via Darmstadt	
1913		Pinkus Krémègne; M. Kiköine, Mané–Katz and C. Soutine arrive in Paris and live at "La Ruche"	First literary publications of Franz Kafka
			Else Lasker-Schüler, lyric poet, publishes *Hebraeische Balladen*
		M. Rothko, age 10, arrives in Portland, Oregon from Russia with his family	
		H. Leivick, Yiddish poet, arrives in U.S.	
		J. Myers exhibits at Armory Show in NYC	
1914	World War I begins		An-Ski publishes "Dos yidische ethnographische program" in *Jewish Academy of Petrograd* concerning his Jewish ethnographic expedition
			Blast, manifesto of Vorticist movement, published in England
1915		Establishment of Ben Uri Society in London	*Menorah Journal* published in NYC
		M. Chagall returns to Vitebsk via Berlin	
		M. Janco arrives in Zurich from Bucharest	
1916		Sholom Aleichem dies in NYC	*Der Jude* a monthly magazine founded by Martin Buber
		E. Lissitsky and I. Ryback explore folk art in the synagogues along the Dnieper River, and copy wall paintings of Mohilev Synagogue	Herman Struck's *Skitzen aus Litauen Weissrussland und Kurland*

Date	History	Culture	Publications
1917	Russian Revolution followed by the abolishment of restrictions affecting the Jews Balfour Declaration	Yiddish State Theatre and Habimah Theatre founded in Moscow Constructivist movement in Russia Painter David Sterenberg returns from Paris to Russia and assumes Directorship of Soviet Commission on Culture	
1918	World War I ends	M. Chagall appointed Commissar and Director of Vitebsk Art Academy	
1919	Pogroms in the Ukraine and Poland	C. Soutine paints in Céret S. Menkes arrives in Paris from Poland M. Beckmann paints *Synagogue* E. Lissitsky appointed Professor at Vitebsk Art Academy Nathan Altman, Art Commissar of Petrograd, designs the festivities for first anniversary of Russian Revolution M. Chagall paints murals for Yiddish State Theatre, Moscow Bauhaus established in Weimar	Hermann Cohen's *Die Religion der Vernunft aus den Quellen des Judentums* published posthumously
1920	Histadrut founded in Palestine (General Federation of Jewish Labor)	M. Ardon enters the Bauhaus M. Lieberman elected President of the Berlin Academy of Art Painter Avigdor Steimatsky arrives in Palestine Ben-Zion emigrates to U.S. from the Ukraine via Vienna	N. Gabo and A. Pevsner publish *Realist Manifesto* in Moscow Herman Struck's *Das Ostjuedische Antlitz*
1921		E. Lissitsky moves to Berlin M. Levanon arrives in Palestine from Hungary C. Gross emigrates from Galicia to U.S. Chaim Bialik, Hebrew poet, leaves Odessa with the help of Maxim Gorky and goes to Berlin	Ludwig Wittgenstein publishes *Tractatus Logico–philosophicos* H. Leivick publishes *Der Goilem*

Date	History	Culture	Publications
1922		Berlin becomes a center for Jewish artists and writers—A. Aberdam, N. Altman, B. Aronson, M. Band, M. Chagall, N. Gabo, I. Kulvianski, L. Pasternak, I. Ryback arrive from the East; L. Lozowick comes from U.S.; Saul Tchernichowsky (Hebrew poet), Vladimir Mayakovsky (Russian poet) move to Berlin A. Manievich emigrates from Kiev to U.S. E. Lissitsky engages in propagandistic activity and publishes with Ilya Ehrenburg *Vesh, Gegenstand, Object* Performance of An-Ski's *The Dybbuk* by Habimah Theatre in Moscow; N. Altman designs sets M. Band moves from Berlin to Paris	Gershom Scholem publishes *Das Buch Bahir*, Leipzig Rachel Wischnitzer publishes *Milgroim-Rimon [Journal of Arts and Letters]* in Yiddish and Hebrew, Berlin
1923		L. Segall emigrates to Brazil A. Aberdam, M. Chagall and L. Pasternak go from Berlin to Paris J. Zaritsky arrives in Palestine from Russia D. Bomberg visits Palestine B. Aronson arrives in U.S. from Kiev via Germany and France *Tower of David* exhibition in Jerusalem includes work of R. Rubin, Nahum Gutman, Israel Paldi, Pinhas Litvinovsky and J. Zaritsky	E. Lissitsky publishes "The Synagogue at Mohilev. Reminiscences," in *Rimon* Henryk Berlewi publishes "Jewish Artists in Contemporary Russian Art, The Russian Art Exhibition in Berlin, 1922," in *Rimon* Nathan Altman publishes *Evreiskaia Grafika*, Berlin
1924	Jewish immigration to U.S. limited by Johnson Act	Chaim Bialik arrives in Tel Aviv L. Pasternak visits Palestine Y. Kovarsky moves to Palestine from Vilna L. Krakauer moves to Palestine from Vienna Jacques Chapiro arrives in Paris	
1925	YIVO founded (Yiddisher Vissenshaftlicher Institut-Yiddish Scientific Institute)	Avraham Melnikoff creates the monument *Roaring Lion* at Tel-Hai in memory of its defenders	
1926		Salo Baron, historian, comes to U.S. from Vienna	

Date	History	Culture	Publications
1926 cont.		L. Gottlieb and A. Mintchine arrive in Paris from Poland and Russia	
		I. Ryback moves to Paris	
		Y. Simon studies in Frankfurt with M. Beckmann	
1927		M. Castel moves to Paris from Jerusalem	Richard Krautheimer, art historian, publishes *Mittelalterliche Synagogen*
1928		E. Lissitsky returns to Russia	Rudolf Hallo publishes *Jüdische Volkskunst in Hessen*
		S. Menkes paints *The Torah* in Paris	
1929	Beginning of the Great Depression in U.S.	The Museum of Modern Art opens in NYC	Ernst Cohen Wiener publishes *Die Jüdische Kunst*
		Discovery of mosaic floor of ancient synagogue of Beth Alpha	
1930		B. Shahn executes drawings for a Haggadah; published in U.S. in 1965	
		Art dealer, Ambroise Vollard commissions M. Chagall to illustrate the Bible	
		J. Pascin commits suicide in Paris	
1931		M. Chagall arrives in Palestine with Jewish writers Chaim Bialik and Edmond Fleg	Founding in Berlin of Schocken Verlag, Jewish-oriented publisher
1932		Founding of The Tel Aviv Museum of Art	*Gazit*, journal for literature and art, published in Tel Aviv
		Discovery of ancient synagogue of Dura Europas by American-French expedition	
1933	Hitler rises to power; establishment of first concentration camp in Nazi Germany—Dachau Public burning in Germany of Jewish books and books by opponents of Nazism	Warburg Bibliothek transferred to London and renamed Warburg Institute	Rudolf Hallo publishes *Jüdische Kunst aus Hessen und Nassau (Jewish Art from Hessen and Nassau)*
		M. Liebermann ousted from Presidency of the Berlin Academy of Art; his paintings removed from all German museums.	
		Establishment of Jewish Museum in Berlin	
		Erwin Panofsky, art historian, arrives in the U.S. from Germany	
		M. Ardon, J. Budko and J. Steinhardt settle in Jerusalem	

Date	History	Culture	Publications
1933 cont.		I. Kulvianski flees Berlin for Palestine	
		J. Adler escapes from Düsseldorf to Paris	
1934		Y. Simon works with Diego Rivera in New York	
1935	Nuremberg Laws proclaimed	J. Adler goes to Warsaw	Rachel Wischnitzer publishes *Gestalten und Symbole der Jüdische Kunst*, Berlin (*Forms and Symbols of Jewish Art*)
	Works Progress Administration sponsored by the U.S. Government; participating American artists include H. Bloom, A. Gottlieb, J. Levine, L. Lozowick, M. Rothko, B. Shahn, M. Siporin, M. Soyer	A. Naton moves from Romania to Palestine	
		Richard Krautheimer, art historian, arrives in U.S.	
1936		Aharon Avni establishes Studio for Painting and Sculpture in Tel Aviv	
		Y. Simon and S. Seba emigrate to Palestine; Simon settles in Kibbutz Gan-Shmuel	
		J. Adler goes to U.S.S.R.	
1937	Buchenwald Concentration Camp established	Nazi exhibition *Entartete Kunst (Degenerate Art)*	Salo Baron publishes *A Social and Religious History of Jews*, New York
	Establishment of "Aliya Beth," illegal immigration to Palestine	Y. Bergner moves from Warsaw to Australia	
		Pablo Picasso paints *Guernica*	
		L. Pasternak goes to England	
1938	*Kristallnacht* ("Night of the Broken Glass"): Nazi anti-Jewish riots in Germany and Austria	Hans Tietze, and E. Conrat Tietze, art historians, emigrate from Austria to U.S.	
		Stephen Kayser, art historian, comes to U.S.	
1939	Soviet-German Pact	Guido Schoenberger, art historian, comes to U.S.	
	Poland invaded; World War II begins	N. Bezem emigrates to Palestine from Germany	
	Establishment of ghettos in Poland	J. Bornfriend flees from Prague to England	
	Beginning of destruction of European Jewish communities	Mark Gertler commits suicide	
1940	Himmler directive to establish concentration camp at Auschwitz	Rachel Wischnitzer comes to U.S.	
		J. Herman flees to England	
	Western Europe invaded by the Nazis	M. Maryan inmate at Auschwitz (to 1945)	

Date	History	Culture	Publications
1940 cont.		J. Lipchitz arrives in New York from Paris	
		S. Bak, age 7, flees Vilna and spends four years hiding in a monastery, and in D.P. camps in Germany after the War	
		Ossip Zadkine, flees Paris for U.S.	
1941	Nazis invade Russia; Japan and U.S. enter World War II	M. Janco settles in Palestine	Gershom Scholem publishes *Major Trends in Jewish Mysticism*, Jerusalem
		J. Adler arrives in England	
		E. Lissitsky dies in Moscow	
1942	Germany adopts policy of "Final Solution" for systematic annihilation of European Jews	E. Brauer, age 13, imprisoned in work camp in Austria (to 1945)	
	Armed resistance in the ghettos of Mir, Lehava and Nieswiez— all in Western Byelorussia		
	The Struma sinks in Black Sea with 769 refugees		
1943	Uprising of Warsaw Ghetto	Otto Freundlich dies in Lublin Concentration Camp	
	Resistance and revolt in ghettos of Vilna, Bialystock and Czestochova	O. Ritterband transported to Auschwitz	
	WPA disbanded in U.S.	F. Hundertwasser, age 14, makes first crayon drawings; sixty-nine of his maternal relatives are deported to Eastern Europe and killed	
		B. Reder emigrates to U.S. from Prague	
		C. Soutine dies in Paris	
1944		Picasso paints *Charnel House* (1944-48)	Jacob Leveen publishes *The Hebrew Bible in Art*
1945	Germany surrenders; World War II ends in Europe	Hendrik Werkman executed by the Nazis in the Netherlands	H. Leivick, Yiddish poet, publishes *In Treblinke bin ikh nit geven (I was not in Treblinka)*
		J. Gurvich works with Joaquin Torres-Garcia, in Uruguay	
		H. Paris enters Buchenwald Concentration Camp as artist-correspondent for *Stars and Stripes* newspaper; starts *Buchenwald* series of graphics	
		Else Lasker-Schüler, German poet, dies in Jerusalem	
1946		Rise of Abstract Expressionism in U.S.	Franz Landsberger publishes *A History of Jewish Art*
1947	Start of mass migration to Israel by Holocaust refugees	Establishment of The Jewish Museum in NYC	Helen Rosenau publishes *A Short History of Jewish Art*

Date	History	Culture	Publications
1947 cont.		Discovery of Dead Sea Scrolls	
		J. Lipchitz creates *Miracle*	
		Artist Ben-Zvi creates monument for the children of the Diaspora in Kibbutz Mishmar Haemek, Israel	
1948	Establishment of State of Israel; War of Independence begins	Architect Percival Goodman with assistance of artists Robert Motherwell, Herbert Ferber and Adolph Gottlieb introduce contemporary art in the Synagogue B'nai Israel in Milburn, New Jersey	Rachel Wischnitzer publishes *The Messianic Theme in the Painting of the Dura Synagogue*
	Actor-director Mikhoels murdered by Russian Secret Police		
		Establishment of New Horizons group in Tel Aviv under leadership of J. Zaritsky and M. Janco	
		N. Rapoport creates *Ghetto Monument* on the site of the Warsaw Ghetto	
		S. Bak goes to Israel	
		B. Newman paints *Onement I*	
1949	Year-long air transfer of ca. 50,000 Jews from Yemen to Israel	Y. Kovarsky moves to NYC from Israel	Karl Schwarz publishes *Jewish Artists of the 19th and 20th Centuries*
		Fima emigrates to Israel from Shanghai	
		A. Ofek arrives in Israel from Bulgaria	
1950	Air transfer of 123,000 Jews from Iraq to Israel	J. Adler dies in Aldbourne, near London	
1951	Over 30 Russian-Jewish writers executed	M. Moreh goes from Baghdad to Israel	
1952	Prague Trials		Kurt Weitzman publishes *The Illustration of Septuagint*
1953	"Doctors' Plot" in USSR	Rudolph Wittkower, art historian, arrives in U.S.	Erwin Goodenough publishes 13 volume *Jewish Symbols in the Greco-Roman Period* (1953-65)
1956		Rico Lebrun paints *Buchenwald Series*	Carl Kraling publishes *The Synagogue,* an investigation of the architecture and wall paintings of Dura-Europos
		E. Brauer entertains Israeli troops during the Sinai campaign	
1957		M. Chagall and J. Lipchitz are commissioned to work on the Church of Assy	Nameni Ernst publishes *L'esprit de l'art juif (The Spirit of Jewish Art)*
1959		J. Epstein sculpts *St. Michael Killing the Devil* for Coventry Cathedral	

Date	History	Culture	Publications
1961			Cecil Roth publishes *Jewish Art, An Illustrated History*
1962		Spread of Pop Art movement in U.S.	
1963		*Monumenta Judaica*—an exhibition of 2000 years of Jewish history and culture on the Rhine, at Cologne Stadtmuseum Artist, Boris Penson arrested and sent to hard labor in USSR	
1964		Opening of The Israel Museum in Jerusalem Moshe Barash establishes art history department at Hebrew University, Jerusalem	Kurt Weitzman publishes *The Question of the Influence of Jewish Pictorial Sources on Old Testament Illustration*
1965	Immigration Act liberalizes quota system in US	D. Karavan creates Memorial monument for Negev Brigade near Beersheba	
1967	Six Day War		L.A. Mayer and Otto Kurz publish *Bibliography of Jewish Art*
1968		L. Klapish moves to Jerusalem from Paris	
1970	Leningrad Trials; Russian Jews agitate for the right to emigrate		
1972		M. Rothko commits suicide	Heinrich Strauss publishes *Die Kunst Der Juden im Wandel der Zeit und Umwelt (The Art of the Jews in differing Periods and Environments)*
1973	Yom Kippur War	E. Brauer acts as war correspondent in Golan Heights L. Baskin illustrates *A Passover Haggadah* J. Lipchitz dies in Capri, Italy and is buried in Jerusalem	Mendel Metzger publishes *La Haggada Enluminée. Etude iconographique et stylistique des manuscrits enluminés et décorés de la Haggada du XIIIe au XVIe siècle (The illuminated Haggadah Iconographic and Stylistic Study of illuminated and decorated manuscripts of the Haggadah from the XIII to the XVI Century)*
1974		J. Gurvich dies in NYC, buried in a kibbutz in Israel Y. Bergner paints mural, *Cycle of Expulsion and Return* at Haifa University	Bezalel Narkiss starts publication of *Journal of Jewish Art* at Spertus College, Chicago Yosef Yerulshami publishes *Haggadah and History*
1975		M. Ardon completes triptych on Yom Kippur War: *Kol Nidrai, Sacrifice, Requiem* H. Paris completes environment *Kaddish for the Little Children*	